Food for Thought

More Home Cooking

- Cheryl D. Batton -

CROQUETTES AND FRITTERS

313.—TO CLARIFY FAT

Melt fat, add one pared and sliced raw potato, a pinch of soda, and a tablespoon of water; heat slowly, and cook until fat stops bubbling; strain through double cheesecloth.

314.—TO TRY OUT FAT

Cut any surplus fat into pieces, put into double boiler, cover, cook slowly until fat is extracted, and strain through double cheesecloth.

315.—CRUMBS FOR FRIED FOOD

Dry left-over bits of bread in a slow oven, put through food chopper, using finest cutter, and sift through a coarse sieve. Keep in covered jars.

316.—EGG FOR DIPPING FRIED FOOD

Break egg into a soup plate or similar shallow dish, beat enough to mix yolk and white, and add one-fourth cup of cold water or one-third cup of milk. Coat food thoroughly to prevent soaking fat.

317.—CHEESE BALLS

> 1½ cups cheese cut fine ¼ teaspoon mustard
> 1 tablespoon flour ¼ teaspoon paprika
> ¼ teaspoon salt Whites of 2 eggs beaten stiff

Mix in order given, shape in balls about one inch in diameter, roll in sifted crumbs, and fry in deep fat until brown. Drain on soft paper, and serve hot. Serve with the salad course or as a savory.

318.—CHEESECROQUETTES

3 tablespoons shortening ¼ teaspoon paprika
1/3 cup bread flour   ¼ teaspoon mustard
1 cup hot milk   Few grains cayenne
¼ teaspoon salt   1 cup cheese cut fine

Melt shortening, add flour; add hot milk, and stir until smooth and thick; add seasonings and cheese, and pour into a shallow dish to cool. Shape into small pyramids, roll in sifted crumbs, dip in egg, and again in crumbs, and fry in deep fat until brown. Serve immediately.

319.—FISHCROQUETTES

2 cups cold flaked fish   Salt and cayenne
1 tablespoon lemon juice 1 cup Croquette Sauce (see No. 192)
Few drops onion juice

Use remnants of baked or boiled fish, sprinkle with lemon and onion juice, dust lightly with salt and cayenne, and mix with sauce. When cold, shape into small croquettes or cutlets, dip in crumbs, egg, and again in crumbs, and fry in hot deep fat one minute.

320.—MEATCROQUETTES

To two cups of cooked meat cut in small pieces add one teaspoon of Worcestershire sauce and a few drops of onion juice; mix with one cup of Croquette Sauce (see No. 192) and put on ice until cold. Shape into small croquettes or cutlets, roll in crumbs, dip in egg, and again in crumbs, and fry in hot deep fat. Any left-over meat may be used.

321.—POTATO AND BEAN CROQUETTES

2 cups cold baked beans   1 tablespoon Worcestershire or Brand's A 1 sauce
1 cup mashed potato   Salt if needed
¼ teaspoon paprika

Press beans through a sieve, add potato and seasonings, mix well, and shape into small pyramids. Roll in crumbs, dip in egg, roll in crumbs again, and fry in hot deep fat. Drain on soft paper, and serve with Tomato Sauce (see No. 203).

322.—RICE CROQUETTES

1 egg slightly beaten   1 teaspoon Worcestershire sauce
¼ teaspoon salt   2 tablespoons cold water
¼ teaspoon onion juice   2 cups cooked rice
1 tablespoon tomato ketchup

Mix in order given; shape into small pyramids, dip in crumbs, egg, and again in crumbs, and fry in hot deep fat.

323.—RICE AND RAISIN CROQUETTES

½ cup rice   1 cup hot milk
1 cup boiling water   1 tablespoon butter
1 teaspoon salt   2 tablespoons sultana raisins

Wash rice, stir into boiling salted water, and boil five minutes, add milk, butter, and raisins, and cook over hot water about twenty-five minutes, or until rice is tender. Shape into small pyramids, dip in egg and crumbs, and fry in hot deep fat. Serve with Currant Jelly Sauce (see No. 608) or Lemon Sauce (see No. 613).

324.—SALMON AND POTATO CROQUETTES

Rinse a can of salmon with boiling water, and separate into flakes; mix with two cups of hot, well-seasoned mashed potatoes, and a tablespoon of finely chopped mixed pickles. Shape into small croquettes, dip in crumbs, egg, and then in crumbs again, and fry in hot deep fat one minute.

325.—SLICED APPLE FRITTERS

1 cup flour 1 egg well beaten
¼ teaspoon salt ½ cup cold water
1 tablespoon sugar 3 tart apples

Mix and sift flour, salt, and sugar; add egg and water, and beat well; pare, core, and cut apples into half-inch slices; dip in batter until well coated, and fry in hot deep fat; drain on soft paper, and dust with powdered sugar. Serve with roast pork or sausage, or serve with a liquid sauce as an entrée or a dessert.

326.—BANANA FRITTERS

1 cup flour 1 egg well beaten
1½ teaspoons baking powder ¼ cup cold water
¼ teaspoon salt 2 bananas
1 tablespoon powdered sugar

Mix and sift dry ingredients, add egg and water, and beat well; press bananas through a sieve, add to batter, and drop from a tablespoon into hot deep fat; drain on soft paper, dust with powdered sugar, and serve with Currant Jelly Sauce (see No. 608), or Lemon Sauce (see No. 613), either as an entrée or as a dessert.

327.—CORN FRITTERS

1 can corn 1 teaspoon salt
½ cup dried and sifted crumbs 1 teaspoon baking powder
1 egg well beaten 1 tablespoon flour

½ cup milk

Chop the corn, and add other ingredients in order given. Drop from a tablespoon into hot deep fat and fry until brown. Or sauté in a hot greased frying pan.

328.—CRANBERRY FRITTERS

1 egg well beaten   1 cup flour
¼ teaspoon salt   1½ teaspoons baking powder
2 tablespoons sugar   ½ cup chopped cranberries
¼ cup water

Mix in order given; drop from a tablespoon into hot deep fat, cook about three minutes, drain on soft paper, and dredge with powdered sugar.

329.—RICE AND CURRANT FRITTERS

1 cup flour   1 egg well beaten
1½ teaspoons baking powder   1/3 cup cold water
1/3 teaspoon salt   1 cup cooked rice
2 tablespoons sugar   2 tablespoons washed currants
¼ teaspoon nutmeg

Mix and sift dry ingredients; add egg and water, and beat well; add rice and currants, and drop from a tablespoon into hot deep fat; drain on soft paper, and serve with Currant Jelly Sauce (see No. 608), Orange Marmalade Sauce (see No. 616), or Lemon Sauce (see No. 613).

330.—SALMON FRITTERS

1-1/3 cups flour   2/3 cup water
¼ teaspoon salt   ¼ teaspoon paprika
2 teaspoons baking powder   ¼ teaspoon onion juice
1 egg well beaten   ½ can salmon chopped fine

Sift flour, salt, and baking powder; add egg, water, and seasonings, and beat well; add salmon, and drop from a tablespoon into hot deep fat; cook until brown, drain on soft paper, and serve with Sauce Tartare (see No. 202) or Tomato Sauce (see No. 203).

331.—DOUGHNUTS

2 cups flour	½ cup sugar
2½ teaspoons baking powder	1 egg well beaten
¾ teaspoon salt	½ cup milk
½ teaspoon nutmeg	1 tablespoon melted shortening

Mix and sift dry ingredients; add egg, milk, and shortening, and mix well; chill, and roll out on a floured board until half an inch thick; cut, and fry in hot deep fat. A little more flour may be necessary, but the dough should be as soft as can be handled easily.

332.—SMALL TEA DOUGHNUTS

Follow recipe for Doughnuts (see No. 331), roll mixture very thin, cut with a two-inch doughnut cutter, fry, and dust with powdered sugar. Or fry the cut-out centers of large doughnuts, and roll in powdered sugar.

333.—FRIED JAM CAKES

Roll doughnut mixture very thin, and cut with a three-inch cookie cutter; put a teaspoon of jam on one half, moisten the edges with water, fold double, press edges firmly together, and fry in hot deep fat. Dust with powdered sugar.

SALADS AND SALAD DRESSINGS

334.—COOKED SALAD DRESSING

1½ cups hot milk 2 tablespoons sugar
2 beaten eggs 2 teaspoons mustard
1 tablespoon salt Dash of cayenne
3 tablespoons flour ½ cup hot vinegar

Mix dry ingredients, add to egg, and stir into the hot milk; add vinegar slowly, and cook over hot water for ten minutes, stirring constantly at first. Cool, put into a preserve jar, cover, and keep in a cool place. Whipped cream may be added, if desired, before using. Allow one cup for the whole recipe. Two tablespoons of melted butter or salad oil may be added, but recipe is very good without either.

335.—COOKED SALAD DRESSING (Evaporated Milk)

½ teaspoon salt 1 beaten egg
1 teaspoon mustard 1 tablespoon melted butter
1½ teaspoons sugar 1/3 cup evaporated milk
1½ teaspoons flour 2/3 cup hot water
Few grains cayenne ¼ cup vinegar

Mix in order given, and cook over hot water for ten minutes, stirring constantly at first.

336.—CURRANT JELLY DRESSING

¼ cup currant or any other tart jelly Juice of ½ lemon

2 tablespoons candied ginger chopped Dash of cayenne
4 tablespoons oil

Melt the jelly, add ginger, cool slightly; add oil, lemon juice, and cayenne.

337.—DEVILLED HAM DRESSING

1 egg ¼ teaspoon salt
1 small can devilled ham 1/8 teaspoon pepper
½ cup vinegar ¼ teaspoon mustard
¼ cup water ¼ teaspoon cornstarch

Beat egg, add ham, vinegar, and water; mix salt, pepper, mustard, and cornstarch; add to ham mixture; and cook over hot water ten minutes.

338.—FRENCH DRESSING

2/3 cup oil ½ teaspoon pepper
1/3 cup vinegar ¼ teaspoon mustard
1¼ teaspoons salt 1 teaspoon powdered sugar

Put the ingredients in a pint preserve jar; fasten the cover, chill, and shake well before using. Keep in the ice-box and use as needed. For use with fruit salad, omit mustard. Curry, Brand's A 1 sauce, Worcestershire sauce, tomato ketchup, or similar condiments may be added in small amounts to vary the flavor.

339.—MAYONNAISE DRESSING

Yolk of 1 egg ½ teaspoon paprika
1 teaspoon salt 1 cup salad oil
½ teaspoon powdered sugar 2 tablespoons vinegar
1 teaspoon mustard 1 tablespoon lemon juice

Beat the egg yolk; add the seasonings; add oil, a few drops at a time, until mixture thickens; mix vinegar and lemon juice, and add in small quantities, alternating with the oil; as the oil thickens the dressing, dilute with the acid, leaving the finished dressing thick. It is important to have ingredients and utensils cold.

340.—POTATOMA YONNAISE

½ cup mashed potatoes ½ teaspoon Worcestershire sauce
2 tablespoons oil   ¼ teaspoon salt
3 tablespoons vinegar   ¼ teaspoon mustard
1 teaspoon horseradish   ¼ teaspoon sugar

Mix in order given and serve with vegetable salad or cold meat.

341.—RUSSIANDRESSING

To Mayonnaise Dressing (see No. 339) add one-third cup of thick chili sauce. Cooked salad dressing may be used in place of mayonnaise.

342.—SOURCREAMDRESSING

½ cup sour cream 1 teaspoon powdered sugar
¼ teaspoon salt   3 tablespoons chili sauce

Beat cream until stiff; add salt, sugar, and chili sauce.

343.—QUICKMA YONNAISE

3 tablespoons butter ½ teaspoon sugar
½ teaspoon salt   3 tablespoons oil
½ teaspoon mustard 1 tablespoon vinegar
¼ teaspoon paprika 1 egg

Cream butter, add seasonings, and when well mixed add oil all at once; mix well, add vinegar; mix well, add the well-beaten egg yolk, and fold in the stiffly beaten white of egg. Do not chill.

344.—UNCOOKED SALAD DRESSING (Condensed Milk)

2 eggs beaten
1 can condensed milk
¼ cup melted butter
1 cup vinegar
1½ teaspoons salt
1½ teaspoons mustard
Dash of cayenne

Mix, and beat with egg beater until thickened.

345.—CHICKEN SALAD

2 cups cold cooked chicken
2 cups celery cut fine
Salad dressing
Lettuce
1 hard-cooked egg

Cut remnants of chicken in small pieces and mix with celery and salad dressing; arrange on lettuce leaves and garnish with dressing and egg thinly sliced. Cabbage and a little celery salt may be used in place of celery.

346.—CORONADO SALAD

1 can tuna fish
2 cups shredded cabbage
1 green pepper cooked and shredded
Cooked Dressing (see No. 334)
2 tablespoons tomato ketchup

Flake fish; shred cabbage very fine; cut pepper in halves, remove seeds, cook in boiling water ten minutes, and shred in inch lengths; mix, arrange on lettuce, and dress with boiled dressing, to which the ketchup has been added. Garnish with parsley or pimiento.

347.—MEAT AND POTATO SALAD

1½ cups cooked meat cut fine   ½ teaspoon salt
1½ cups cooked potato cut fine 2 tablespoons finely chopped pickle
½ cup celery cut fine   Salad dressing

Mix in order given, cover with dressing, and garnish with sliced pickles and celery tops. White cabbage may be used in place of celery.

348.—SALMON SALAD

1 can salmon   2 finely chopped pickles
1 cup cooked potato cubes   Cooked Dressing (see No. 334)
1 cup shredded lettuce   Lettuce

Rinse salmon with boiling water, and separate into flakes; mix with potato, lettuce, and pickles, arrange on lettuce, and cover with dressing. Garnish with sliced hard-cooked egg and parsley.

349.—SHRIMP SALAD

1 pint cooked shrimps   ¾ cup salad dressing
1 cup chopped white cabbage 1 head lettuce
2 tablespoons capers

Clean shrimps and break in pieces, reserving a few of the largest; mix with cabbage, capers, and dressing, and serve in lettuce nests. Garnish with whole shrimps. Canned shrimps may be used.

350.—TUNA FISH SALAD

1 can tuna fish   Salad dressing
2 cups cooked potato cubes Lettuce
½ cup cooked beet

Flake tuna fish, mix with potatoes cut into fine cubes, and the beet cut into inch shreds; arrange on lettuce or any crisp salad green; and dress with Cooked Dressing (see No. 334) or Mayonnaise (see No. 339).

351.—BAKED BEAN SALAD

2 cups cold baked beans   1 cup Cooked Dressing (see No. 334)
1 cup cooked potato cubes   2 tablespoons tomato ketchup
½ cup chopped cooked beet 2 tablespoons chopped pickle

Mix beans, potato, and beets; add ketchup and pickle to dressing, mix with vegetables, and serve on lettuce or any crisp salad green. Garnish with radishes.

352.—BERMUDA ONION SALAD

6 Bermuda onions   ½ bay leaf
2 quarts boiling water Small piece lemon peel
1 dozen pepper corns Lettuce
4 cloves   French Dressing (see No. 338)
½ teaspoon salt

Peel and quarter onions, and cook in boiling water with seasonings until tender; drain, cool, arrange on lettuce, and cover with dressing. Garnish with red radishes.

353.—CABBAGE AND BEET SALAD

3 cups shredded cabbage 2 tablespoons vinegar
3 beets finely chopped ¼ teaspoon white mustard seed
¼ teaspoon salt Cooked Dressing (see No. 334)

Mix cabbage, beets, salt, vinegar, and mustard seed; arrange on small white cabbage leaves, and dress with cooked dressing. Garnish with parsley.

354.—CABBAGE AND CRANBERRY SALAD

3 cups finely shredded white cabbage ½ cup chopped cranberries
½ cup finely shredded celery

Mix with Cooked Dressing (see No. 334), and garnish with celery tops and whole cranberries.

355.—CELERY ROOT SALAD

2 cups Creamed Celery Root (see No. 253) 1 cup shredded white cabbage
1 cup chopped apple

Mix, and serve on lettuce with Cooked Dressing (see No. 334) or Mayonnaise Dressing (see No. 339).

356.—DUTCH POTATO SALAD

6 boiled potatoes ¼ teaspoon celery seed
½ onion finely chopped ¼ teaspoon white mustard seed
1 teaspoon salt ¼ cup bacon fat

¼ teaspoon pepper   ½ cup hot vinegar

Cut potatoes into half-inch cubes; add onion, salt, pepper, celery, and mustard seed; heat bacon fat, add vinegar, and pour over potatoes; let stand until cold, and serve on any crisp salad green. Garnish with pickled beet.

357.—LEEK SALAD

Cut leeks in half-inch slices and cook in boiling salted water until tender; drain, chill, and serve on lettuce with French Dressing (see No. 338); sprinkle with chopped parsley and paprika.

358.—PEPPER AND CABBAGE SALAD

½ small white cabbage   1 red pepper
1 green pepper   Salad dressing

Shred cabbage into fine inch shreds; remove seeds and veins from peppers, and cut into fine shreds. Mix with dressing and arrange on small inner cabbage leaves. Garnish with parsley and strips of red pepper.

359.—POTATO SALAD

6 potatoes   ½ teaspoon salt
1 onion   ½ teaspoon paprika
½ teaspoon celery seed   Salad dressing
¼ teaspoon mustard seed

Pare potatoes, cut in halves, and cook in boiling salted water with the onion until tender; cool, cut in half-inch cubes, add seasonings, and mix with dressing. Cover with dressing, and garnish with parsley, red beets, or cooked carrot. Devilled Ham Dressing (see No. 337) is excellent with potato salad.

360.—SWEET POTATO SALAD

3 cups of cooked sweet potato cubes
1 cup white cabbage or celery finely chopped
2 tablespoons vinegar
4 tablespoons oil
1 tablespoon Worcestershire sauce
½ teaspoon salt

Mix and serve on heart cabbage leaves, and garnish with parsley and pickles.

361.—SAMOSET SALAD

Arrange lettuce in salad bowl, cover with slices of pickled beets, and sprinkle thickly with cottage cheese. Cover with dressing made of three tablespoons each of beet vinegar and oil, one-fourth teaspoon salt, and one-eighth teaspoon pepper.

362.—SPANISH SALAD

1 head of lettuce
2 cups of half-inch cubes of bread
1 Spanish onion chopped fine
1 cucumber sliced
3 tomatoes quartered
French Dressing (see No. 338)
2 sliced pickles

Shred the coarser leaves of the lettuce, and arrange in salad bowl on heart leaves; cover with bread cubes, sprinkle with onion, add cucumber and tomatoes, and pour French dressing over all. Garnish with pickles.

363.—SPANISH ONION AND TOMATO SALAD

1 head lettuce
4 mild onions
2 ripe tomatoes
1 green pepper
French Dressing (see No. 338)

Wash and dry lettuce, and arrange in salad bowl; peel onions, cut in very thin slices, and put on lettuce; peel and slice tomatoes, and place on onions; cut pepper in thin slices, remove seeds and veins, and place on tomatoes;

cover with French dressing, and serve very cold with brown bread sandwiches.

364.—TOMATO JELLY SALAD

1 can tomatoes   1/8 teaspoon soda
½ onion   Dash of cayenne
4 cloves   ½ bay leaf
1 teaspoon salt   ½ box gelatine
1 teaspoon sugar   ½ cup cold water

Cook tomatoes and seasonings for twenty minutes; soak gelatine in cold water for a few minutes; add to tomato, and stir until dissolved; press through a sieve, and fill individual molds, which have been garnished with a slice of hard-cooked egg. Serve on lettuce with any dressing preferred. A small amount of clear jelly may be made by allowing mixture to drip through a jelly bag. Put into very small molds, and use as a garnish for cold meat or salads. The pulp left in the bag will make excellent soup.

365.—VEGETABLE SALAD (Cooked)

1½ cups potatoes   French Dressing (see No. 338)
1 cup beets   ¼ teaspoon onion juice
¾ cup white turnip   1 bouillon cube
½ cup peas

Cut potatoes, beets, and turnips into half-inch cubes, and mix with peas; dissolve bouillon cube in one tablespoon of boiling water, and add with onion juice to dressing. Arrange vegetables on any crisp salad green, and pour dressing over them.

366.—APPLE AND MINT SALAD

2 cups finely cut apple   4 tablespoons oil
2 tablespoons chopped mint   Few grains cayenne

2 tablespoons lemon juice 1 head lettuce
Few gratings lemon rind

Mix the mint, lemon juice, and rind, cover, and let stand for half an hour; add oil and cayenne, and pour over apple. Serve on lettuce and garnish with sprigs of mint.

367.—BANANA AND APPLE SALAD

Peel and slice three bananas; pare, core, and slice four apples; arrange on lettuce, and cover with Currant Jelly Dressing (see No. 336).

368.—BANANA AND PEANUT SALAD

Peel and scrape bananas, cut crosswise into three pieces, roll in finely chopped peanuts, and serve on lettuce with French Dressing (see No. 338).

369.—BELLEVUE SALAD

1 cup cottage cheese ¼ cup French Dressing (see No. 338)
½ cup peanut butter 1 large red apple
½ teaspoon salt Lettuce leaves

Mix cheese, butter, salt, and dressing until well blended; core apples, cut in one-third-inch slices, and cover each slice with cheese mixture forced through a rose tube; arrange on lettuce, and serve with French dressing.

370.—CREAM CHEESE SALAD

Force cream cheese through potato ricer, arrange lightly on lettuce leaves, and dress with a French Dressing (see No. 338), to which two tablespoons of chili sauce have been added.

371.—FROZEN CREAM CHEESE

Mash a cream cheese, season with paprika and salt, moisten with cream, and beat until smooth; pack into individual paper cases, put into a tightly covered tin, and pack in equal parts of salt and ice for three hours. Serve on lettuce with French Dressing (see No. 338), and garnish with bits of currant jelly or Mock Bar-le-Duc Currants (see No. 666).

372.—JELLIED WALDORF SALAD

½ package gelatine 1 cup celery shredded
½ cup cold water ½ cup nut meats chopped
1 cup boiling water Lettuce
¼ cup sugar 6 pimolas sliced
¼ cup lemon juice Mayonnaise
2 cups apple chopped

Soak gelatine in cold water five minutes, add boiling water, sugar, and lemon juice; chill until it begins to stiffen; add apples, celery, and nuts; turn into individual molds, and chill. Serve on lettuce, and garnish with pimolas and mayonnaise.

373.—ORANGE AND CRESS SALAD

1 bunch water cress 4 seedless oranges
1 head romaine French Dressing (see No. 338)

Pick over, wash, and dry cress; wash and dry romaine, and arrange in salad bowl; peel and cut oranges in thin slices, and arrange over romaine; put cress around edge of bowl, and cover all with French dressing made with lemon juice instead of vinegar.

374.—PEAR SALAD

5 pears 1 teaspoon Jamaica ginger
Lettuce 1 teaspoon powdered sugar
4 tablespoons oil ½ teaspoon paprika

2 tablespoons lemon juice

Pare, quarter, and core fruit; wash and dry lettuce; shred finely the outer leaves, and arrange on the heart leaves; cut quarters of pears lengthwise, place on lettuce, and cover with dressing made of oil, lemon juice, and seasonings. The pears should not be too ripe.

375.—PINEAPPLE, CHEESE, AND DATE SALAD

For each person allow two lettuce leaves, one slice of pineapple, and three dates stuffed with cream cheese. Cut the pineapple in cubes and place on the lettuce; cut dates in halves lengthwise, remove stones, stuff with cream cheese, and arrange on pineapple; sprinkle cheese with paprika, and dress all with French Dressing (see No. 338).

376.—PINEAPPLE AND COTTAGE CHEESE SALAD

Arrange slices of pineapple on crisp lettuce; in the center of each slice place a cottage cheese ball rolled in chopped nut meats; dress with French Dressing (see No. 338).

YEAST BREADS, MUFFINS, AND ROLLS

377.—WHITE BREAD

1 cup scalded milk	2½ teaspoons salt
1 cup boiling water	½ yeast cake
1 tablespoon sugar	¼ cup lukewarm water
2 tablespoons shortening	6 to 7 cups flour

Put liquid, sugar, shortening, and salt in the mixing bowl; when lukewarm add the yeast cake (which has been dissolved in lukewarm water); add flour and knead well. The exact amount of flour will depend upon the quality; but enough should be used to make a smooth, soft dough which after kneading is not sticky. Cover, and let rise in a warm room until double in bulk; cut down, knead well, and shape into loaves; cover, let rise until double in bulk, and bake in a hot oven about fifty minutes. To hurry the rising of the bread increase the quantity of yeast. Bread mixed with two yeast cakes may be made and baked in about three hours.

378.—BRAN BREAD (Yeast)

½ cup boiling water	½ yeast cake
½ cup scalded milk	¼ cup lukewarm water
2 tablespoons shortening	1 cup entire wheat flour
2 tablespoons molasses	1 cup white flour
1½ teaspoons salt	2 cups bran

Mix water, milk, shortening, molasses, and salt; when lukewarm add yeast cake dissolved in lukewarm water, add flour sifted, and bran, and mix with liquid to a soft dough; let rise until light, cut down, and knead into small loaves, using more bran if necessary to prevent sticking; let rise until nearly double, and bake in hot oven about fifty minutes.

379.—ENTIRE WHEAT BREAD

Follow recipe for White Bread (see No. 377), using four cups of entire wheat flour and two or more cups of white flour. Molasses may be used in place of sugar.

380.—DATE BREAD (Not Kneaded)

1 cup scalded milk	½ yeast cake
1 cup boiling water	¼ cup lukewarm water
4 cup molasses	4 cups entire wheat flour
2 tablespoons shortening	1¼ cups white flour
2 teaspoons salt	1 cup dates cut in pieces

Mix milk, water, molasses, shortening, and salt; when lukewarm, add yeast, dissolved in lukewarm water, and flour; mix, and beat well; let rise until double in bulk; add dates, beat well, turn into two greased bread pans, let rise until light, and bake one hour. The oven should be hot for the first fifteen minutes, and then the heat should be reduced.

381.—FRIED BREAD

Cut raised bread dough into pieces the size of a small egg, flatten with the rolling pin, cover, let rise until light, and fry in deep fat about three minutes.

382.—GRAHAM AND CORN BREAD

1 cup corn meal	¼ cup molasses
1 cup boiling water	½ yeast cake
1 cup scalded milk	¼ cup lukewarm water
2 tablespoons shortening	4 cups Graham flour

2½ teaspoons salt

Pour boiling water over corn meal; mix well, add milk and shortening; when lukewarm add salt, molasses, and yeast dissolved in lukewarm water; add flour, beat well, and let rise until double in bulk; beat again, pour into two greased bread pans, let rise until light, and bake about fifty minutes. The oven should be hot for the first fifteen minutes, and then the heat reduced.

383.—IRISH BREAD

1 quart bread dough ¼ cup sugar
1/3 cup shortening   1 cup raisins seeded and chopped

Knead shortening, sugar, and raisins into dough; shape into two round loaves, let rise, brush with milk, and bake in hot oven about forty minutes.

384.—OATMEAL BREAD

1 cup rolled oats   ½ yeast cake
½ cup corn meal   ¼ cup lukewarm water
1½ teaspoons salt   ½ cup molasses
1 tablespoon shortening 4 cups flour
2 cups boiling water

Mix oats, corn meal, salt, and shortening; add boiling water, and let stand one hour; add yeast dissolved in lukewarm water, molasses, and flour. Mix well, cover, and let rise until double in bulk; beat well, turn into two greased pans, let rise, and bake in a hot oven about fifty minutes.

385.—RYE BREAD

1 cup scalded milk   ½ yeast cake
1 cup boiling water   ¼ cup lukewarm water
2 tablespoons shortening 3 cups rye flour

3 tablespoons molasses 3 to 4 cups white flour
2 teaspoons salt

Mix; let rise and bake the same as White Bread (see No. 377).

386.—SHREDDED WHEAT BREAD

2 shredded wheat biscuit 1 tablespoon shortening
1 cup hot milk ½ yeast cake
1 cup hot water ¼ cup lukewarm water
½ cup molasses 6 cups entire wheat flour
1 tablespoon salt

Crumble the biscuit; add milk, water, molasses, salt, and shortening; when lukewarm add yeast cake dissolved in lukewarm water, and sifted flour; knead well, cover and let rise until double in bulk; cut down, shape into loaves or biscuit, put into greased pans, let rise until light, and bake in a hot oven about fifty minutes for loaves, and twenty-five minutes for biscuit. This makes one loaf and one pan of biscuit. A little more or less flour may be needed.

387.—BUNS

1 cup scalded milk ½ yeast cake
1/3 cup shortening ¼ cup lukewarm water
¼ cup sugar ½ cup currants
1 teaspoon salt 3½ cups flour

Mix milk, shortening, sugar, and salt; when lukewarm, add yeast dissolved in lukewarm water; add currants, and flour enough to knead (a little more or less than the three and one-half cups may be required); let rise until double in bulk; knead, and shape into small round buns; place in a greased baking pan two inches apart, and let rise until light; brush with milk, dust with powdered sugar, and bake in a hot oven about twenty minutes.

388.—CRESCENTS

Use Parker House Roll mixture (see No. 389) or any bread dough into which more shortening has been kneaded; roll out half an inch thick, cut into four-inch squares, and cut squares in halves diagonally; brush with melted shortening, and roll firmly, beginning with the diagonal edge. Curve into crescent shape, place on greased baking sheet, let rise until light, and bake in a hot oven about fifteen minutes.

389.—PARKER HOUSE ROLLS

2 cups milk
1/3 cup shortening
1 teaspoon salt
2 tablespoons sugar
1 yeast cake
¼ cup lukewarm water
6 to 7 cups flour

Scald milk; add shortening, salt, and sugar; when cool add yeast dissolved in water; stir in two cups of flour, cover, and let rise until double in bulk; add enough flour to form a soft dough; knead well, and let rise again; cut down with a knife; roll out on lightly floured bread board until about half an inch thick; cut with small round cutter, brush with butter, and fold double; put on baking sheet, cover, and let rise until light, brush with milk, and bake in hot oven about twelve minutes.

390.—SHAMROCK ROLLS

To one quart of bread dough add one-fourth cup of melted shortening and two tablespoons of sugar. Knead well, and shape into small balls about the size of a pecan nut; grease muffin tins, put three balls in each, let rise until light, and bake in a hot oven about fifteen minutes.

391.—SWEDISH COFFEE ROLLS

1 cup scalded milk ½ yeast cake
1/3 cup shortening ¼ cup lukewarm water

1 teaspoon salt	3½ cups flour
¼ cup sugar	1 teaspoon cinnamon
1 egg well beaten	2 tablespoons sugar

Scald milk, add shortening, salt, and sugar; when lukewarm add egg, yeast dissolved in water, and flour, of which a little more or less may be required; knead well, cover, and let rise until double in bulk; knead again; roll on a floured board until about one-fourth of an inch thick, brush with melted shortening, and sprinkle with cinnamon mixed with sugar; fold dough into three layers, cut in strips three-quarters of an inch thick; twist each strip, and shape like a figure eight, pressing the ends firmly in place; put on a greased baking sheet, let rise until light, and bake in a hot oven twenty minutes. Spread with a thin coating of plain icing.

392.—RAISED MUFFINS

½ cup boiling water	1 egg
½ cup scalded milk	¼ yeast cake
1 teaspoon salt	¼ cup lukewarm water
2 tablespoons sugar	2½ cups flour
2 tablespoons shortening	

Pour water and milk over salt, sugar, and shortening; when cool add beaten egg, yeast dissolved in water, and flour; beat well and let rise over night; beat again; fill greased muffin pans two-thirds full, let rise, and bake in a hot oven thirty minutes. Or place greased muffin rings on a hot greased griddle, fill two-thirds full, and cook on top of range about twenty minutes, turning when half cooked.

393.—RAISED CORN MUFFINS

1 cup scalded milk	¼ yeast cake
4 tablespoons shortening	¼ cup lukewarm water
4 tablespoons sugar	1 cup corn meal
1 teaspoon salt	1½ cups flour

Add shortening, sugar, and salt to milk; when lukewarm add yeast dissolved in water, corn meal, and flour; beat well, let rise over night; beat well, half fill greased muffin rings, let rise until nearly double, and bake in hot oven half an hour.

394.—RAISED DATE MUFFINS

Follow recipe for Date Bread (see No. 380); half fill greased muffin tins, let rise until light, and bake in a hot oven twenty-five minutes. Figs cut in small pieces may be used instead of dates.

395.—RAISED OATMEAL MUFFINS (Uncooked Oats)

1 cup rolled oats	1 egg
1 cup scalded milk	¼ yeast cake
2 tablespoons shortening	¼ cup lukewarm water
1 teaspoon salt	2½ cups flour
¼ cup molasses	

Pour hot milk over oats, add shortening; when lukewarm add salt, molasses, egg well beaten, and yeast cake dissolved in lukewarm water; beat well, and add flour; beat well, and let rise over night; beat again, and half fill greased muffin pans; let rise until nearly double, and bake in a hot oven half an hour.

396.—RAISED ROULETTES

Roll out to one-half inch thickness any roll or soft raised bread mixture; brush with melted butter, and spread with cinnamon and sugar, fruit, or any of the fillings used for Baking Powder Roulettes (see No. 447). Roll like a jelly roll until dough is about two and one-half inches in diameter, cut in half-inch slices with a sharp knife, place on greased sheet two inches apart, let rise until light, and bake in a hot oven twenty minutes.

BAKING POWDER BREADS, MUFFINS, AND BISCUIT[10]

397.—BAKING POWDER

1 pound 2 ounces *pure* cream of tartar   ¼ pound cornstarch
½ pound cooking soda

Mix and sift thoroughly four times, and store in closely covered jars.

398.—BARLEY BREAD

2 cups barley meal   1 teaspoon salt
1 cup Graham flour   6 teaspoons baking powder
1 cup white flour   2 cups milk
2 tablespoons sugar

Sift dry ingredients together, and mix well with milk; turn into a greased bread tin, let stand fifteen minutes, and bake in a moderate oven fifty minutes. Raisins, dates, figs, or nuts may be added.

399.—BRAN BREAD

2 cups bran   5 teaspoons baking powder
2 cups entire wheat flour ½ cup molasses
1 teaspoon salt   ¾ cup water
½ teaspoon soda   ¾ cup milk

Sift flour, salt, soda, and baking powder, and add to bran; add molasses and liquid, and beat well; turn into a greased bread pan; let stand fifteen minutes, and bake in a moderate oven one hour.

400.—DATE BREAD

1 cup corn meal
1 cup entire wheat flour
1 cup white flour
1½ teaspoons salt
¼ teaspoon soda
5 teaspoons baking powder
¼ cup molasses
1 cup dates stoned and cut in pieces
½ cup nut meats chopped
1 egg well beaten
1¼ cups milk

Mix and sift dry ingredients; add other ingredients in order given; mix well, turn into a greased bread pan, cover with a cloth, let stand fifteen minutes; bake in a moderate oven fifty minutes.

401.—DARK NUT BREAD

¼ cup sugar
¾ cup hot water
½ cup molasses
¾ cup milk
2 cups entire wheat flour
1 cup bread flour
5 teaspoons baking powder
1½ teaspoons salt
½ teaspoon soda
¾ cup nut meats finely chopped

Mix in order given, sifting dry materials together before adding. Turn into a greased bread pan, let stand fifteen minutes, and bake in a moderate oven one hour.

402.—QUICK RAISIN BREAD

2½ cups entire wheat flour
½ cup fine corn meal
6 teaspoons baking powder
1 teaspoon salt
¼ cup sugar
1 beaten egg
1¼ cups milk
1 cup seeded raisins cut in halves

Mix and sift dry ingredients; add egg, milk, and raisins, and mix well; put into a greased bread pan, cover, and let stand fifteen minutes; bake in a moderate oven about fifty minutes. One cup of finely chopped nuts may be added.

403.—BREAD CRUMB BROWN BREAD

1½ cups dried sifted crumbs ½ cup corn meal
1 cup boiling water 1 cup Graham flour
½ cup molasses ¾ teaspoon salt
1 cup milk 1½ teaspoons soda

Put crumbs in mixing dish, add boiling water, and let stand ten minutes; add molasses, milk, and the dry ingredients sifted together. Steam the same as Steamed Indian Date Bread (see No. 404).

404.—STEAMED INDIAN DATE BREAD

1½ cups corn meal 2/3 cup molasses
1 cup rye meal 1 cup water
½ cup flour 1 cup milk
1½ teaspoons soda 1 cup dates
1 teaspoon salt

Mix and sift dry ingredients, add molasses, liquid, and dates which have been stoned and cut in pieces. Pour into greased one-pound baking powder boxes, and steam steadily for one and three-quarters hours. Or pour into a large greased mold and steam for three hours.

405.—CORN BREAD (without Eggs)

¾ cup corn meal ½ teaspoon salt
¾ cup flour ¾ teaspoon soda
2 tablespoons sugar 1½ cups buttermilk or sour milk

Mix and sift dry ingredients, add buttermilk gradually, and beat well; pour into well-greased shallow pan, and bake in hot oven twenty minutes.

406.—COUNTRY CORN BREAD

¾ cup corn meal	1/3 teaspoon salt
¾ cup flour	1 beaten egg
3 teaspoons baking powder	¾ cup milk and water mixed
1 tablespoon sugar	2 tablespoons melted bacon fat

Mix in order given, beat well, and bake in a well-greased shallow pan in a hot oven about twenty minutes. Half of the egg will make a very good corn bread. Left-over pieces may be split, lightly buttered, and browned in the oven.

407.—CORN MUFFINS

1 cup corn meal	2 tablespoons sugar
1 cup flour	1 beaten egg
4 teaspoons baking powder	1 cup milk and water mixed
½ teaspoon salt	4 tablespoons melted shortening

Mix in order given, beat well, and bake in greased gem pans in hot oven twenty minutes.

408.—CORN AND RICE MUFFINS

1 cup cooked rice	1 tablespoon sugar
2/3 cup hot milk	1 egg
½ cup corn meal	½ cup flour
2 tablespoons bacon fat	3 teaspoons baking powder
½ teaspoon salt	

Pour hot milk over rice, and work with a fork to separate grains; add corn meal, bacon fat, salt, and sugar; when cool add egg well beaten, flour, and baking powder; beat well; bake in well-greased muffin pans in hot oven twenty minutes.

409.—CUSTARD CORN CAKE

½ cup corn meal 1 cup sour milk
½ cup flour 1 egg
2 tablespoons sugar 2 tablespoons melted shortening
½ teaspoon salt ½ cup sweet milk
½ teaspoon soda

Mix and sift dry ingredients; add sour milk and egg well beaten, and beat thoroughly; melt shortening in an earthen baking dish, pour in batter, pour the sweet milk over it, and bake in a hot oven twenty-five minutes. Cut in wedge-shaped pieces for serving.

410.—MOLASSES CORN BREAD

1 cup corn meal 1 egg
1 cup flour ¼ cup molasses
4 teaspoons baking powder 1 cup water
½ teaspoon salt 2 tablespoons melted bacon fat

Mix and sift dry ingredients; add egg well beaten, molasses, water, and bacon fat; beat well, pour into a well-greased shallow pan, and bake about twenty minutes in a hot oven.

411.—RHODE ISLAND CORN CAKE

1 cup white corn meal 2 tablespoons sugar
1 cup flour 1 egg
4 teaspoons baking powder ¼ cup melted shortening
½ teaspoon salt 1 cup milk

Mix and sift dry ingredients; add egg yolk well beaten, shortening, and milk; beat well; fold in the stiffly beaten white of egg, and bake in a greased, shallow pan in hot oven about twenty minutes.

2 cups bran
1 cup flour
½ teaspoon salt
1 teaspoon soda
½ cup molasses
1¾ cups milk
1 tablespoon melted shortening

Mix in order given; beat well, and bake in moderate oven about twenty-five minutes. These muffins are moist, keep well, and may be reheated successfully in a covered pan, either over steam or in the oven.

414.—CAMBRIDGE MUFFINS

¼ cup shortening
¼ cup sugar
1 egg
¾ cup milk
2 cups flour
4 teaspoons baking powder
¼ teaspoon salt

Cream the shortening; add the sugar and egg well beaten; beat well, add the milk, flour, baking powder, and salt, which have been sifted together; beat again, and bake in hot greased muffin pans twenty minutes in a moderate oven.

415.—CHEESE MUFFINS

Use recipe for Plain Muffins (see No. 419) or any muffin recipe, omitting the sugar; cut cheese in half-inch cubes, and place three or four pieces on top of each muffin before baking.

416.—CRANBERRY MUFFINS

Follow recipe for Cambridge Muffins (see No. 414), and add one cup of cranberries coarsely chopped.

417.—CRUMB MUFFINS

1 cup dried and sifted bread crumbs 1 egg

1 tablespoon shortening
1 tablespoon sugar
½ teaspoon salt
½ cup boiling water

½ cup milk
¾ cup flour
3 teaspoons baking powder

Mix crumbs, shortening, sugar, salt, and boiling water; when cool add the egg well beaten, the milk, flour, and baking powder; beat well and bake in greased muffin pans twenty minutes in a moderate oven.

418.—DATE MUFFINS

To recipe for Plain Muffins (see No. 419) or Cambridge Muffins (see No. 414) add one cup dates, stoned and cut in small pieces.

419.—PLAIN MUFFINS

2 cups flour
4 teaspoons baking powder
½ teaspoon salt
2 tablespoons sugar

1 egg
1 cup milk
2 tablespoons melted shortening

Mix and sift dry ingredients; add egg well beaten, milk, and shortening; beat well, and bake in greased muffin pans in moderate oven twenty minutes. For fruit muffins add one cup of figs, dates, or cooked prunes cut in pieces.

420.—RYE MUFFINS

1 cup rye flour
1 cup white flour
½ teaspoon salt
4 teaspoons baking powder

2 tablespoons molasses
1 egg
2 tablespoons melted shortening
1 cup milk

Mix and sift dry ingredients, add molasses, egg well beaten, shortening, and milk; beat well, half fill greased muffin tins, and bake in moderate oven twenty minutes.

421.—SOUR MILK MUFFINS

1½ cups flour 1 egg
1 tablespoon sugar 1 cup thick sour milk
½ teaspoon soda 2 tablespoons melted shortening
½ teaspoon salt

Mix and sift dry ingredients; add egg well beaten, sour milk, and shortening; beat quickly, and bake in greased muffin pans in moderate oven twenty minutes.

422.—BUTTERMILK MUFFINS

Follow recipe for Sour Milk Muffins (see No. 421), using buttermilk instead of sour milk.

423.—SALLY LUNN

2 cups flour 2 eggs
4 teaspoons baking powder 1 cup milk
½ teaspoon salt ¼ cup melted shortening
2 tablespoons sugar

Mix and sift dry ingredients; add eggs well beaten, milk, and shortening; beat thoroughly, pour into shallow greased pan, and bake in a moderate oven twenty minutes.

424.—BAKING POWDER BISCUIT

2 cups flour 2 tablespoons shortening
4 teaspoons baking powder ¾ cup milk
1 teaspoon salt

Mix and sift dry ingredients, rub in shortening until fine and crumbly, and add milk to form a soft dough; a little more or less may be required, according to the brand of flour used. Roll out on a slightly floured board until three-fourths of an inch thick, cut with small cutter, place on greased pan an inch apart, and bake in hot oven twelve minutes. For soft biscuit with little crust, place close together in the pan, and bake five minutes longer. Left-over biscuit may be split, lightly buttered, and browned in the oven.

425.—CORN MEAL ROLLS

1 cup corn meal
1 cup flour
4 teaspoons baking powder
½ teaspoon salt
3 tablespoons bacon fat
¾ cup milk

Mix and sift dry ingredients; rub in shortening with finger tips; add milk, and mix thoroughly; roll lightly, on a floured board, to a thickness of one-half inch; cut with biscuit cutter, brush with milk or water, and fold double. Bake in hot oven fifteen minutes.

426.—BACON SANDWICH ROLLS

Follow recipe for Corn Meal Rolls (see No. 425), putting a piece of cooked bacon on half of roll before folding.

427.—DATE ROLLS

Use recipe for Baking Powder Biscuit (see No. 424), roll out one-half inch thick, and cut in rounds with three-inch cutter; spread with soft butter, sprinkle with cinnamon and sugar, and put a date, split lengthwise and stoned, on half of each roll; fold over, press edges firmly together, brush with milk, and bake in hot oven fifteen minutes. Allow one-half teaspoon cinnamon to two tablespoons sugar. Cooked and stoned prunes or chopped figs may be used instead of dates.

428.—QUICK COFFEE CAKE

¼ cup shortening	2½ cups flour
¼ cup sugar	5 teaspoons baking powder
1 egg	½ teaspoon salt
1 cup milk and water mixed	2 tablespoons sugar
½ cup seedless raisins	1 teaspoon cinnamon

Cream the shortening and sugar; add egg well beaten, milk, raisins, flour, baking powder, and salt; spread in a greased shallow pan, brush with melted butter, and sprinkle with cinnamon and sugar; bake in hot oven fifteen to twenty minutes.

429.—QUICK DROP BISCUIT

Use recipe for Baking Powder Biscuit (see No. 424), increasing the milk to one cupful; drop from a tablespoon on a greased pan two inches apart, and bake in a hot oven ten minutes; or half fill greased muffin tins, and bake twelve minutes.

430.—ENTIRE WHEAT BISCUIT

Follow directions for Baking Powder Biscuit (see No. 424), using entire wheat flour in place of white flour, and adding one tablespoon of molasses.

431.—FRUIT TEA BISCUIT

To recipe for Quick Drop Biscuit (see No. 429) add one chopped apple, one-half cup of seeded and chopped raisins, two tablespoons of washed currants, and two tablespoons of sugar. Put into hot greased muffin pans, and bake in a hot oven fifteen minutes. Serve for tea, or with a hot liquid sauce for dessert.

432.—GRAHAM BISCUIT

1 cup Graham flour	½ teaspoon salt
½ cup fine corn meal	2 tablespoons shortening

½ cup bran   1 tablespoon molasses
4 teaspoons baking powder ¾ cup milk

Mix dry ingredients without sifting; rub in shortening with finger tips; add molasses and milk; mix well; roll, cut, and bake as directed for Baking Powder Biscuit (see No. 424).

433.—JAM ROLLS

2 cups flour   2 tablespoons shortening
4 teaspoons baking powder 1 egg
1 teaspoon salt   2/3 cup milk
1 tablespoon sugar

Sift together flour, baking powder, salt, and sugar; rub in shortening with finger tips until mealy; add beaten egg and milk, and mix with a knife to a soft dough; roll out one-third of an inch thick, and cut with a round cutter; put a teaspoon of jam on each, moisten the edges with water, fold over, and press firmly together; make two cuts on top so that jam will show, brush with milk, and bake in hot oven fifteen minutes.

434.—POTATO SCONES

2 cups flour   1 cup mashed potato
½ teaspoon salt   2 tablespoons shortening
4 tablespoons baking powder ¾ cup milk

Sift flour, salt, and baking powder; add potato and shortening, and work in with finger tips; add milk, and mix to a soft dough with a knife; roll out three-quarters of an inch thick on floured board, cut with biscuit cutter, and cook on hot greased griddle about twenty minutes, turning over when half cooked. Split, butter, and serve hot.

435.—SCOTCH SCONES

1 cup fine oatmeal   4 teaspoons baking powder
¾ cup scalded milk   1 teaspoon salt
2 tablespoons shortening 2 tablespoons sugar
1 cup flour

Pour hot milk over oatmeal, mix well, add shortening, and let stand until cold; mix and sift flour, baking powder, salt, and sugar; add to oatmeal, and mix well; roll out three-fourths of an inch thick, cut in rounds, and cook on a greased griddle about twenty minutes, turning when half cooked.

WITHOUT BAKING POWDER OR YEAST

436.—POPOVERS

1 cup flour   1 cup milk
¼ teaspoon salt 1 teaspoon melted butter
1 egg

Sift flour and salt; beat egg very light, and mix with milk; mix gradually with flour; add melted butter, and beat two minutes with a strong egg beater; pour into hot greased popover cups or pans, and bake in a hot oven twenty to thirty minutes, according to size of pans. The mixture should be very cold, and the pans and oven very hot.

437.—ENTIRE WHEAT POPOVERS

¾ cup entire wheat flour 1 cup milk
¼ cup corn meal   1 egg
¼ teaspoon salt   1 teaspoon melted butter

Follow directions for mixing and baking Popovers (see No. 436).

438.—GRAHAM POPOVERS

Follow recipe for Entire Wheat Popovers (see No. 437), except that Graham flour should be used in place of entire wheat.

439.—BREAKFAST PUFFS

1 cup entire wheat flour 1 cup ice water
¼ teaspoon salt

Sift flour and salt, add ice water gradually, and beat three minutes with strong egg beater; bake in hot iron pans in very hot oven twenty minutes.

440.—MARYLAND BEATEN BISCUIT

2 cups flour   2 tablespoons shortening
½ teaspoon salt Cold water

Sift flour and salt, rub in shortening with tips of fingers, and add enough cold water to make a stiff dough; knead until smooth, and beat with the rolling-pin fifteen minutes, or until dough blisters; roll out about one-third of an inch thick, cut with a small round cutter, prick with a fork, place on a greased baking pan, and chill in the ice-box for half an hour; bake about twenty-five minutes, having the oven very hot for the first ten minutes. A biscuit brake may be used instead of rolling-pin.

SHORTCAKES AND ROULETTES

441.—SHORTCAKE

1½ cups flour 3 tablespoons shortening
3 teaspoons baking powder 2/3 cup milk
1/3 teaspoon salt

Mix and sift flour, baking powder, and salt; rub in shortening with finger tips; add milk, and mix well with a knife. Spread in two greased layer-cake pans, patting with the back of a tablespoon until pans are evenly filled. Bake in a hot oven twelve minutes. If individual shortcakes are preferred, roll, cut with a biscuit cutter, and bake quickly about fifteen minutes; split, and put filling between and on top.

442.—APPLE AND CRANBERRY SHORTCAKE

4 apples 2 teaspoons cornstarch
½ cup cranberries 2 tablespoons sultana raisins
½ cup water A few gratings of orange peel
½ cup sugar

Core and slice apples, add cranberries and water; cook ten minutes, and press through a sieve; mix sugar and cornstarch, stir into fruit; add raisins and grated rind, and simmer ten minutes; spread between and on top of shortcake, and garnish with a few raisins.

443.—BANANA SHORTCAKE

Prepare Shortcake (see No. 441), slice two small bananas over layer of hot shortcake, and sprinkle with lemon juice and powdered sugar; put on upper layer, cover with two more sliced bananas, sprinkle with lemon juice and sugar, and garnish with bits of jelly.

444.—DATE AND APPLE SHORTCAKE

½ pound dates 1/3 cup sugar
4 tart apples ¼ teaspoon nutmeg
½ cup water

Wash and stone dates, and cut in pieces; pare, core, and slice apples; simmer with dates, water, sugar, and nutmeg until thick enough to spread. Spread between and on top of Shortcake (see No. 441).

445.—PRUNE AND APPLE SHORTCAKE

1½ cups prunes 2 teaspoons cornstarch
2 apples pared and chopped Grated rind of ½ lemon
1/3 cup sugar

Wash prunes and soak over night in cold water to cover; cook in same water until tender; remove stones and return to water in which they were cooked; add apple, and heat to boiling point; add sugar mixed with cornstarch, and grated rind; cook about ten minutes, or until thick. Prepare recipe for Shortcake (see No. 441), and put sauce between and on top.

446.—STRAWBERRY SHORTCAKE

Prepare Shortcake (see No. 441); hull one box of berries, and save out a few of the largest; mash the remainder, and add about one-half cup of sugar; pour half of berries over hot shortcake, put on second layer, and cover with remaining berries; garnish with large whole berries, and serve with or without plain cream. Blackberry, Raspberry, Currant, or Blueberry Shortcake may be made in the same way, the amount of sugar necessary depending upon the acidity of the fruit.

447.—ROULETTES

Use recipe for Baking Powder Biscuit (see No. 424), turn on floured board, roll out one-half inch thick, brush with soft butter, and spread with any of the following mixtures; then roll firmly like a jelly roll until dough is about two and one-half inches in diameter; cut in one-half-inch slices with a sharp knife, place on a greased sheet two inches apart, and bake in a hot oven twelve minutes.

Cheese Roulettes: Spread with four tablespoons of grated cheese seasoned with salt and cayenne.

Devilled Ham Roulettes: Spread lightly with devilled ham, or any finely chopped and well-seasoned meat.

MarmaladeRoulettes: Spread lightly with any marmalade or jam.

Peanut Butter Roulettes: Spread with peanut butter and dust lightly with salt; sprinkle with salt before baking.

Raisin and Nut Roulettes: Spread with mixture of one-half cup of seeded and chopped raisins and one-fourth cup finely chopped nut meats.

FruitRoulettes: Spread with currants, chopped citron, figs, dates, prunes, or candied ginger.

SANDWICHES AND TOASTS

448.—BAKED BEAN AND LETTUCE SANDWICHES

Press cold baked beans through a sieve; spread bread with butter, cover with a lettuce leaf, cover lettuce with beans, and sprinkle beans with chopped mustard pickle. Cover with a second piece of buttered bread. Brown bread or any dark bread may be used.

449.—CELERY AND EGG

> 1 cup chopped celery ¼ cup mayonnaise
> 1 hard-cooked egg

Put celery and egg through the food chopper, using finest cutter; add mayonnaise, and salt if necessary; spread between thin slices of buttered brown bread.

450.—CHEESE AND NUT SANDWICHES

Mix equal parts of grated American cheese and chopped nut meats; season with salt and cayenne, moisten with cream, and spread between thin buttered slices of bread.

451.—CHEESE CLUB SANDWICHES

Cut bread in half-inch slices, remove crusts, spread with Mustard Butter (see No. 459), cover with a lettuce leaf, spread with salad dressing, cover with cheese cut in thin slices, sprinkle with chopped mixed pickles, and cover with a second slice of bread spread with mustard butter. Cut in quarters diagonally.

452.—CHICKEN SANDWICHES (Open)

1 cup finely chopped chicken Dash of celery salt
½ teaspoon salt ¼ cup salad dressing
Dash of cayenne

Season the chicken, add the dressing, and beat well. Butter circles of white bread, and spread with the chicken, mounding it in the center. Garnish with slices of pimolas.

453.—GIBLET SANDWICHES

Cook giblets until tender, put through food chopper, and mix with salad dressing. Spread between thin slices of buttered bread. A lettuce leaf may be added.

454.—HAM AND CHEESE SANDWICH (Hot)

Spread thin buttered slices of stale bread with finely chopped ham; cover with thin slices of American cheese; cover with another slice of bread spread with ham, and sauté in a little butter until brown. These sandwiches may be toasted if preferred.

455.—MARSHMALLOW SANDWICHES

Toast marshmallows and press while hot between ginger snaps, vanilla wafers, or butter thins.

456.—MOCK CRAB SANDWICHES

1 cup young America cheese cut fine 1 teaspoon anchovy paste
3 tablespoons milk ½ teaspoon paprika

Mix cheese to a paste with milk, anchovy, and paprika; spread between thin buttered slices of brown bread.

457.—PEANUT SANDWICH FILLING

Put freshly roasted peanuts through the food chopper, using the finest cutter, season with salt, and mix to a smooth paste with cream; or dilute peanut butter with a little milk until of consistency to spread easily.

458.—RAISIN BREAD AND CHEESE SANDWICHES

Cut raisin bread in thin slices, and spread with Cottage Cheese (see No. 234) mixed to a paste with a little fruit juice or cream. Trim neatly and cut in triangles.

459.—MUSTARD BUTTER

¼ cup butter
1 teaspoon dry English mustard
A few drops of vinegar or lemon juice
A few grains of cayenne

Cream the butter, add the mustard and seasonings, and beat well.

460.—BREWIS

1 cup brown bread crumbled
1 cup white bread crumbled
1 cup milk
1/8 teaspoon salt
1 tablespoon butter

Put crumbled bread in a shallow pan in a slow oven until browned; put in a saucepan with milk, salt, and butter, and cook about ten minutes, beating well. Serve as cereal or dessert. Left-over corn bread or muffins may be used.

461.—BROWN BREAD TOAST WITH CHEESE AND BACON

Toast brown bread, or crisp in the oven, dip quickly into hot salted water, and arrange on serving dish. Make a Sauce for Cream Toast (see No. 464), add to it one-half cup of cheese cut fine, pour over toast, and put a piece of crisp bacon on each piece.

462.—CELERY TOAST

2 cups celery cut in half-inch pieces 1/3 cup flour
3 cups hot stock or water   ¼ cup milk
Salt   6 slices toast
1/8 teaspoon pepper

Cook celery in stock or water about half an hour, or until tender; add salt (if necessary), pepper, and flour mixed to a paste with the milk; stir until thickened, and simmer fifteen minutes; pour over toast, and garnish with toast points and celery tips. Use the coarser unbleached pieces of celery for cooking.

463.—CREAM TOAST

Cut six slices of bread in halves, toast slowly, or put into a moderate oven until light brown and crisp, dip each piece into Sauce for Cream Toast (see No. 464), and put into a covered serving dish; pour over remaining sauce, and cover for two or three minutes before serving.

464.—SAUCE FOR CREAM TOAST

2 cups milk   ½ teaspoon salt
3 tablespoons flour 1 tablespoon butter
¼ cup cold water

Scald the milk; mix the flour to a smooth paste with water, add to milk and stir until thickened; cook over hot water fifteen minutes, stirring occasionally; add salt and butter, and pour over toast.

465.—CHEESE TOAST

To recipe for Cream Toast (see No. 463) add one-half cup of either soft cheese cut fine or grated cheese.

466.—CINNAMON TOAST

Cut stale bread into thin slices, remove crusts, and cut in halves; toast evenly, and spread first with butter, then with honey, and dust with cinnamon. Serve very hot.

467.—FRENCH TOAST

1 egg slightly beaten ¾ cup milk or coffee
¼ teaspoon salt   4 slices bread
1 tablespoon sugar

Mix egg, salt, sugar, and liquid in a shallow dish; soak bread in mixture, and cook on a hot, greased griddle until brown, turning when half cooked. Serve plain or spread with jam.

468.—GOLDENROD HAM TOAST

Follow recipe for Cream Toast (see No. 463); to the sauce add one-half cup finely chopped ham and the finely chopped whites of two hard-cooked eggs. When toast is in the serving dish, sprinkle with the hard-cooked yolks rubbed through a sieve.

469.—SUNDAY TOAST

Cut whole wheat bread into four one-inch slices, remove crusts, butter, and cut bread into three strips; mix one-third cup of brown sugar, one teaspoon of cinnamon, two tablespoons of seeded and chopped raisins, and a tablespoon of milk; spread paste on bread, and bake in a hot oven until brown. Serve hot.

470.—TOMATO CREAM TOAST WITH EGG

½ can tomato	1/3 cup cold water
1/3 teaspoon salt	2/3 cup hot milk
1/3 teaspoon soda	1 tablespoon butter
1 teaspoon sugar	2 hard-cooked eggs
4 tablespoons flour	6 slices toast

Simmer tomato for fifteen minutes and press through a sieve; add salt, soda, and sugar; heat to boiling point, and thicken with flour mixed to a smooth paste with cold water; cook five minutes, and add hot milk and butter. Dip toast in sauce, place on platter, cover with remaining sauce, and garnish with egg cut into eighths lengthwise.

471.—TO FRESHEN STALE LOAF BREAD, ROLLS, MUFFINS, OR DOUGHNUTS

Dip quickly into cold water, put in a paper bag, fold top of bag firmly, and place in a hot oven until heated through.

472.—BUTTERED CRUMBS

Melt two tablespoons of butter, stir in one-half cup of coarse, dried bread crumbs until butter is absorbed.

473.—CROUSTADES

Cut stale bread in slices about an inch and a half thick, remove crusts, and cut in rounds, squares, triangles, or any shape desired; remove the centers, using a small, sharp knife, and leaving a wall one-third of an inch thick; brush with melted butter, and brown in oven; or fry, inverted, in hot, deep fat.

474.—CROUTONS

Cut stale bread in one-third-inch slices, cut slices into cubes, and brown in the oven or fry in deep fat. Cold toast may be used instead of bread.

GRIDDLE CAKES, WAFFLES, AND SIRUPS

476.—PLAIN GRIDDLE CAKES

1½ cups flour
3 teaspoons baking powder
½ teaspoon salt
1 tablespoon sugar
1 egg well beaten
1 tablespoon melted shortening
½ cup milk
¾ cup water

Mix and sift dry ingredients; add egg well beaten, shortening, and liquid; beat well, and cook on a hot griddle. The cakes should be small and should be served very hot with butter and sirup.

477.—SOUR MILK GRIDDLE CAKES

2 cups flour
½ teaspoon salt
1 teaspoon soda
2 teaspoons sugar
2 cups thick sour milk
1 egg well beaten

Mix and sift dry ingredients, add milk and egg, and beat well; cook the same as Plain Griddle Cakes (see No. 476).

478.—CORN MEAL GRIDDLE CAKES

1½ cups corn meal
½ cup flour
4 teaspoons baking powder
¾ teaspoon salt
1 tablespoon molasses
1 egg well beaten
¾ cup milk
¾ cup water
1 tablespoon melted shortening

Mix in order given, beat well, and cook on a hot, greased griddle. If all of the batter is not needed at once, cover what is left, and keep in a cold place; add one-half teaspoon of baking powder, and beat vigorously before using; or half of the recipe may be used and the extra half egg used in some other way.

479.—DRIED CRUMB GRIDDLE CAKES

1 cup dried and sifted bread crumbs 2 tablespoons sugar
1 cup flour
1 egg
½ teaspoon salt
1¼ cups milk
4 teaspoons baking powder

Mix and cook according to directions for Plain Griddle Cakes (see No. 476). Half milk and half water may be used.

480.—RICE GRIDDLE CAKES

1 cup cooked rice 2 teaspoons baking powder
1 egg well beaten 1 tablespoon sugar
1 cup milk   ½ teaspoon salt
1 cup flour   Few gratings nutmeg

Mix rice and egg thoroughly with a fork, add milk, and dry ingredients mixed and sifted together; beat well, and cook the same as Plain Griddle Cakes (see No. 476).

481.—RAISED BUCKWHEAT CAKES

1 cup boiling water   ¼ cup lukewarm water
½ teaspoon salt   1 cup buckwheat flour
1 tablespoon molasses ¼ cup white flour
½ yeast cake   ½ teaspoon soda

Mix boiling water, salt, and molasses, and when lukewarm add yeast dissolved in lukewarm water; add gradually to flour, and beat well; let rise over night, add soda, beat well, and cook the same as Plain Griddle Cakes (see No. 476).

482.—WAFFLES

1½ cups flour
½ teaspoon salt
3 teaspoons baking powder
1 teaspoon sugar
1 egg well beaten
1 cup milk
3 tablespoons melted shortening

Mix and sift dry ingredients; add egg, milk, and shortening, and beat well; cook in a hot, well-greased waffle iron.

483.—CORN MEAL WAFFLES

Follow recipe for Oatmeal Waffles (see No. 484), using one cup of corn meal mush in place of oatmeal.

484.—OATMEAL WAFFLES

1 cup cooked oatmeal
Yolks of 2 eggs
1 cup milk
2 tablespoons melted shortening
1 cup entire wheat flour
2 teaspoons baking powder
½ teaspoon salt
1 tablespoon sugar
Whites of two eggs

Mix oatmeal and yolks of eggs (which have been beaten very light) until there are no lumps in the mixture; add milk, shortening, and dry ingredients sifted together; beat well, and fold in the stiffly beaten whites of eggs. Cook in a hot, well-greased waffle iron.

485.—RICE WAFFLES

To recipe for Waffles (see No. 482) add one-half cup of cooked rice, mixing the rice thoroughly with the beaten egg before adding.

486.—BROWN SUGAR SIRUP

Boil one cup of brown sugar and one-half cup of water until the consistency of thick maple sirup. Serve hot or cold.

487.—CIDER SIRUP

1½ cups cider 1 cup sugar

Heat cider, add sugar, and boil until a thick sirup is formed, skimming when necessary. Serve hot or cold.

488.—LEMON SIRUP

Boil one cup of sugar, one-half cup of water, and one tablespoon of lemon juice until the consistency of thick maple sirup; add one teaspoon of butter, and serve hot.

489.—ORANGE SIRUP

¾ cup orange juice Grated rind ½ orange
1 cup sugar

Boil orange juice and sugar until mixture has the consistency of thick maple sirup, add rind, and serve hot or cold.

CAKES AND COOKIES[11]

490.—APPLE SAUCE CAKE (without Butter, Eggs, or Milk)

1 cup unsweetened apple sauce	¼ teaspoon salt
½ cup melted shortening	1 teaspoon cinnamon
1 cup sugar	½ teaspoon nutmeg
1 teaspoon soda	¼ teaspoon clove
2 cups flour	1 cup raisins seeded and chopped

Mix in order given, sifting dry ingredients together, beat well, pour into a deep pan, and bake about one hour in a slow oven.

491.—CANADA WAR CAKE (without Butter, Eggs, or Milk)

1 cup brown sugar	1 teaspoon cinnamon
¼ cup shortening	½ teaspoon mace
1 cup boiling water	¼ teaspoon clove
2 cups seeded raisins	1 teaspoon soda
½ teaspoon salt	2 cups flour

Mix sugar, shortening, water, raisins, and salt; boil five minutes; cool, and add spices, soda, and flour sifted together; beat well; pour into a greased, paper-lined bread pan, and bake in a slow oven one hour.

492.—DATE CAKE

1/3 cup melted shortening 1¾ cups flour
1¼ cups brown sugar 3½ teaspoons baking powder
1 egg unbeaten ½ teaspoon mace
½ cup milk 1 cup dates stoned and chopped

Mix in order given, and beat vigorously for three or four minutes; bake in two layer-cake pans in a moderate oven for twenty-five minutes; when partly cool spread with tart jelly, and sprinkle top layer with powdered sugar.

493.—FUDGE CAKE

¼ cup shortening ½ cup milk
1 cup brown sugar 1½ cups flour
1 square chocolate 3 teaspoons baking powder
1 egg well beaten ¼ teaspoon salt

Cream shortening, add sugar, and beat well; add chocolate melted and egg; beat again; add milk; add flour, baking powder, and salt sifted together; beat for two minutes. Pour into two greased layer-cake pans, and bake in a moderate oven about eighteen minutes. Fill, and spread top with Fudge Filling (see No. 533).

494.—OLD-FASHIONED PORK CAKE

½ pound fat salt pork ¼ pound citron shredded
1 cup boiling water 1 nutmeg grated
1 cup molasses   2 teaspoons cinnamon
1 cup sugar   ½ teaspoon cloves
2 eggs beaten   ½ teaspoon allspice
½ pound raisins   1 teaspoon soda
½ pound currants 4 cups flour

Put pork through meat chopper, using finest cutter; add boiling water and let stand fifteen minutes; add molasses, sugar, eggs, and fruit, and mix well;

add dry ingredients, which have been sifted together; beat well; pour into two deep greased and paper-lined pans; and bake in a slow oven two hours. This cake keeps well if stored in a covered stone crock. It may be reheated in the top of double boiler, and served hot with pudding sauce.

495.—ONE-EGG CAKE

2 tablespoons butter 1½ cups flour
½ cup sugar 2½ teaspoons baking powder
1 egg Grated rind of 1 lemon
½ cup milk

Cream the butter, add the sugar and the well-beaten egg; beat thoroughly, add the other ingredients in the order given, and bake in a moderate oven about half an hour.

496.—ORANGE CAKE

¼ cup shortening 1½ cups flour
1 cup sugar 2½ teaspoons baking powder
1 egg Grated rind ½ orange
½ cup milk

Cream the shortening, add sugar and egg well beaten; add milk, flour, baking powder, and rind; beat well, and bake in two layer pans about twenty minutes in a moderate oven. Fill and cover top with Orange Icing (see No. 527).

497.—PLAIN CAKE

1/3 cup shortening 1-2/3 cups flour
1 cup sugar 3 teaspoons baking powder
2 eggs Few grains salt
½ cup milk ½ teaspoon lemon extract

Beat shortening and sugar until light and creamy; add eggs well beaten, flour, baking powder, salt, and extract; beat well, pour into a greased and papered cake pan, and bake about half an hour in a moderate oven, or in two layer-cake pans about twenty minutes. This is an excellent foundation cake for use with various flavorings, icings, and fillings.

498.—SPICE CAKE (without Eggs)

1/3 cup shortening	1½ teaspoons cinnamon
1 cup sugar	¾ teaspoon nutmeg
1 cup sour milk	¼ teaspoon cloves
2 cups flour	¼ teaspoon salt
1 teaspoon soda	1 cup raisins seeded and chopped

Cream shortening and sugar, add sour milk; add dry ingredients sifted together; beat well; add raisins, pour into a greased shallow pan, and bake half an hour in a moderate oven. Dust with confectioners' sugar or cover with plain icing.

499.—WHITE CAKE

Whites of 2 eggs	3 teaspoons baking powder
Melted butter	7/8 cup sugar
Milk	½ teaspoon almond extract
1½ cups flour	

Break the whites of eggs into a measuring cup; add melted butter to half fill cup; add milk to fill cup. Mix and sift flour, baking powder, and sugar; combine mixtures, add flavoring, and beat for five minutes. Bake in a shallow cake pan half an hour, or in muffin tins about twenty minutes, in a moderate oven.

500.—SPONGE CAKE (Hot Water)

Yolks of 2 eggs	Whites of 2 eggs

¼ cup hot water 1 cup flour
7/8 cup sugar 2 teaspoons baking powder
Grated rind 1 lemon ¼ teaspoon salt

Beat the yolks of eggs until thick and light, add the water and sugar, and beat three minutes with the egg beater; add the lemon rind and the whites stiffly beaten; sift flour, baking powder, and salt, and fold in carefully. Pour into a shallow greased pan, and bake in a moderate oven twenty-five minutes.

501.—VELVET SPONGE CAKE

2 eggs ½ cup pastry flour
1 cup sugar 2 teaspoons baking powder
1/8 teaspoon salt Grated rind 1 lemon
¼ cup potato flour 1/3 cup hot milk

Beat eggs until very light, add sugar gradually, and continue beating with the egg beater; mix and sift salt, flour, and baking powder; add half to the eggs and sugar, and beat well; add rest of flour, and beat again; add rind and milk, and beat hard; pour into a deep pan, and bake forty minutes in a slow oven.

502.—CREAM PIE

Follow rule for Jelly Roll Cake (see No. 503); bake in two layers, and fill with Cream Filling (see No. 531).

503.—CAKE FOR JELLY ROLL OR CHARLOTTE RUSSE

2 eggs 1 cup flour
1 cup powdered sugar 1½ teaspoons baking powder
1/3 cup hot water ¼ teaspoon salt

Beat the eggs very light, add sugar gradually, and continue beating; add water, flour, baking powder, and salt. Pour into a greased, paper-lined dripping pan and bake in a moderate oven about fifteen minutes. The cake should be about half an inch thick when baked. Trim off the edges, spread with jam or jelly, and roll firmly; wrap in a paper napkin to keep in shape. For Charlotte Russe cut cake into pieces to fit paper cases, and fill with Charlotte Russe Mixture (see No. 562).

504.—CHOCOLATE MARSHMALLOW ROLL

To recipe for Jelly Roll (see No. 503) add two squares of melted chocolate. Bake as for jelly roll, trim edges, spread with Marshmallow Filling (see No. 534), and roll the same as jelly roll.

505.—HOT WATER GINGERBREAD (without Egg)

¼ cup shortening   1 teaspoon soda
1 cup dark molasses ½ teaspoon salt
½ cup boiling water 1½ teaspoons ginger
2 cups bread flour   ½ teaspoon cinnamon

Mix shortening, molasses, and water; add dry ingredients sifted together, and beat well. Pour into greased muffin pans and bake in a moderate oven twenty minutes; or pour into a greased shallow pan and bake twenty-five minutes.

506.—HOT WATER GINGERBREAD (with Egg)

1/3 cup beef drippings 2¾ cups flour
2/3 cup boiling water   1 teaspoon soda
1 cup dark molasses   ½ teaspoon salt
1 egg well beaten   1½ teaspoons ginger

Pour boiling water over shortening, add molasses and egg; mix and sift dry ingredients, add to first mixture, and beat well. Pour into a shallow, greased cake pan, and bake in a moderate oven twenty-five minutes.

507.—SOUR MILK GINGERBREAD

2 cups flour   1 cup molasses
1½ teaspoons soda   1 cup thick sour milk
1 teaspoon ginger   1 egg well beaten
¼ teaspoon salt

Mix and sift dry ingredients, add molasses, milk, and egg, and beat well; pour into a greased pan, and bake in a moderate oven twenty-five minutes.

508.—GINGER APPLE CAKE

Follow any recipe for gingerbread, bake in two layers, and put Apple Filling (see No. 529) between layers and on top.

509.—GINGER GEMS

½ cup molasses   1½ cups flour
¼ cup brown sugar   1 teaspoon soda
¼ cup shortening   1 teaspoon ginger
½ cup boiling water   ½ teaspoon cinnamon
1 beaten egg   ¼ teaspoon salt

Mix in order given, sifting the dry ingredients together; beat well, pour into greased muffin tins, and bake in a moderate oven twenty minutes.

510.—BRAN DROP COOKIES

1 cup bran   ¼ teaspoon clove
½ cup flour   ¼ cup molasses
¼ teaspoon salt   ¼ cup sugar
¼ teaspoon soda   ¼ cup melted shortening

½ teaspoon cinnamon ¼ cup milk

Mix in order given, drop from tablespoon, two inches apart, on greased pan, and bake in a hot oven twelve minutes.

511.—CHEESE DROPS

2 tablespoons butter
¼ cup grated cheese
¼ cup dried and sifted crumbs
¼ teaspoon salt
1/8 teaspoon paprika
1/8 teaspoon mustard
Few grains cayenne
Whites of 2 eggs

Cream butter and cheese together; mix crumbs with seasonings and add to cheese; fold in the stiffly beaten whites of eggs. Drop from a teaspoon on a greased baking sheet about two inches apart, and bake in a moderate oven about twelve minutes. Serve with soup or salad.

512.—CHEESE WAFERS

1 cup flour
¼ teaspoon salt
½ teaspoon paprika
1 tablespoon shortening
½ cup grated cheese
¼ cup cold water

Mix and sift flour, salt, and paprika; rub in shortening with finger tips; add cheese and mix to a stiff paste with cold water; roll out very thin, cut with a small round cutter, place on a greased baking sheet, and bake in a moderate oven five or six minutes. Serve with salad or soup.

513.—CHOCOLATE COOKIES

2 squares chocolate
½ cup shortening
1 cup brown sugar
1 egg well beaten
¼ cup milk
2 cups flour
2½ teaspoons baking powder
½ teaspoon salt
½ teaspoon cinnamon

Put chocolate with shortening in mixing bowl and place over hot water until melted; add other ingredients in order given. Chill, roll thin, and cut with fancy cutter. Bake in a moderate oven about ten minutes.

514.—GINGER WAFERS

½ cup shortening ¼ teaspoon salt
1 cup brown sugar 1¼ teaspoons ginger
2¼ cups bread flour ½ cup milk
½ teaspoon soda

Cream shortening and sugar; sift soda, salt, and ginger with flour, and add alternately with milk; chill; roll thin on baking sheet; mark in squares, and bake in a moderate oven eight or ten minutes. Remove from pan while warm.

515.—MARSHMALLOW WAFERS

Arrange thin crackers or wafers on a baking sheet, place a marshmallow on each one, and bake in a moderate oven for a few minutes until marshmallows melt; into each one press half a nut meat, raisin, cherry, or a bit of candied fruit.

516.—MOLASSES BROWNIES

1/3 cup shortening 1 beaten egg
1/3 cup sugar ½ teaspoon baking powder
1/3 cup molasses 1 cup flour
2 squares melted chocolate ¾ cup chopped nut meats

Cream the shortening, add other ingredients in order given, drop from spoon on greased pan, and bake about twelve minutes in a moderate oven.

517.—OATMEAL MACAROONS

1 egg
½ cup sugar
1 tablespoon melted butter
1 cup rolled oats
1/3 cup shredded coconut
½ teaspoon salt

Beat egg until light, add other ingredients in order given, beat well, and drop from spoon on greased pan; bake about fifteen minutes in a moderate oven.

518.—PEANUT MACAROONS

White of 1 egg   1 cup powdered sugar
1/8 teaspoon salt 1 cup finely chopped peanuts

Add salt to the egg, and beat until stiff; add sugar and nuts, and mix well; drop from a teaspoon on a greased baking sheet two inches apart, and bake in a slow oven about fifteen minutes.

519.—RAISIN DROP COOKIES

3 tablespoons shortening 1 cup flour
½ cup brown sugar   2 teaspoons baking powder
1 egg well beaten   1 teaspoon cinnamon
2 tablespoons milk   ½ cup raisins seeded and chopped

Cream the shortening and sugar; add egg and milk, and beat well; add flour, baking powder, and cinnamon sifted together; add raisins; beat well, drop from a teaspoon two inches apart on a greased baking sheet, and bake in a moderate oven about twelve minutes.

520.—WALNUT WAFERS

2 eggs   ¼ teaspoon salt
1 cup brown sugar   ¼ teaspoon baking powder
½ cup flour   ¾ cup chopped nut meats
¼ teaspoon cinnamon

ICINGS AND FILLINGS

521.—BOILED ICING[12]

1/3 cup boiling water White of 1 egg
1 cup sugar 1 teaspoon vanilla
1/8 teaspoon cream of tartar

Boil water and sugar to 240° F., or until the sirup forms soft ball when tried in cold water; add cream of tartar and vanilla, and pour slowly upon the stiffly beaten white of egg, beating constantly until thick enough to spread without running. For caramel flavor melt one-third of the sugar first.

522.—CARAMEL ICING

1 cup brown sugar 1 teaspoon butter
1/3 cup milk Few grains salt

Put ingredients in saucepan, and boil to 240° F., or until a soft ball can be formed when tested in cold water. Beat until creamy, and spread while warm. Chopped nut meats may be added.

523.—CHOCOLATE ICING

2 squares chocolate Confectioners' sugar
¼ cup boiling water ½ teaspoon vanilla

Melt chocolate, add boiling water, and mix well; add confectioners' sugar until of right consistency to spread; add vanilla and beat well. Coffee may be used in place of water.

524.—COCOA ICING

1 tablespoon butter 2 tablespoons cocoa
2 tablespoons milk Confectioners' sugar

Heat butter and milk in a saucepan, remove from fire, add cocoa, and enough confectioners' sugar to thicken. About one cup of sugar will be required.

525.—COFFEE ICING

Follow directions for Boiled Icing (see No. 521), using strong coffee in place of water. Or to recipe for Quick Icing (see No. 528) or Cream Icing (see No. 526) add one teaspoon of instantaneous coffee.

526.—CREAM ICING

1¼ cups confectioners' sugar ¼ teaspoon vanilla
Heavy cream

Sift sugar and add cream until of right consistency to spread (about two tablespoons); add flavoring, and beat well.

527.—ORANGE ICING

Juice of ½ orange Confectioners' sugar
Grated rind of ¼ orange

Mix sugar with orange juice and rind until icing is firm enough to spread.

528.—QUICK ICING

1 tablespoon butter Confectioners' sugar
2 tablespoons boiling water ¼ teaspoon flavoring

Pour boiling water over butter; stir in sugar enough to thicken; add extract, and beat well before spreading. (A little more than one cup of sugar will usually be required.)

529.—APPLE FILLING

3 baked apples 1 cup confectioners' sugar
White of 1 egg

Press apples through a sieve; beat white of egg until stiff; add half of sugar, and beat well; add apple and remaining sugar gradually, and beat until very light. Spread between layers and on top of cake. Two tablespoons of tart jelly may be beaten with the apple.

530.—COFFEE CREAM FILLING

Follow recipe for Cream Filling (see No. 531), but use one-half cup strong coffee in place of one-half cup of milk. Or add one teaspoon of instantaneous coffee to the recipe.

531.—CREAM FILLING

1½ cups milk   1/8 teaspoon salt
1 cup sugar   1 egg slightly beaten
¼ cup cornstarch 1 teaspoon flavoring

Scald milk, mix sugar, cornstarch, salt, and egg; add to milk, and cook over hot water, stirring constantly until mixture thickens; cook fifteen minutes, stirring occasionally. Cool and flavor before spreading.

532.—DATE AND FIG FILLING

1 cup figs   ½ cup boiling water
1 cup dates   Juice ½ lemon
½ cup sugar

Wash, dry, and chop figs; wash, dry, stone, and chop dates; mix fruit with sugar, water, and lemon juice, and cook over hot water until thick enough to spread.

533.—FUDGE FILLING

1½ cups brown sugar 1/3 cup milk
1 tablespoon butter   Few grains salt
1 square chocolate   ½ cup nut meats chopped

Put sugar, butter, chocolate, milk, and salt in a saucepan; heat slowly to boiling point, and boil to 240° F., or until a soft ball can be formed when tested in cold water; remove from fire, add nuts, and beat until smooth and creamy.

534.—MARSHMALLOW FILLING

1 cup sugar   ½ pound marshmallows
1/3 cup boiling water 1 teaspoon vanilla

Boil sugar and water to 240° F., or until a soft ball can be formed when tested in cold water; soften marshmallows over hot water, add sirup, and when partly cooled add vanilla and beat until stiff enough to spread. Chopped nuts, dates, figs, raisins, or candied fruits may be added.

535.—MOCHA FILLING

2 tablespoons hot black coffee ½ teaspoon vanilla
1 tablespoon butter   1 cup confectioners' sugar
2 tablespoons cocoa

Mix coffee, butter, cocoa, and vanilla, and add sugar enough for mixture to spread without running.

536.—ORANGE FILLING

HOT DESSERTS

538.—APPLE ROULETTES

Use recipe for Baking Powder Biscuit (see No. 424); roll dough very thin, brush with melted butter, and spread with one cup of chopped apple, mixed with one-fourth cup of sugar, and one teaspoon of cinnamon; roll firmly like a jelly roll, cut in three-fourths-inch slices, place in buttered pan, and bake in a hot oven fifteen minutes. Serve with hot liquid sauce.

539.—DUTCH APPLE CAKE

1½ cups flour	½ cup milk
3 teaspoons baking powder	2 tablespoons melted shortening
½ teaspoon salt	3 apples
3 tablespoons sugar	2 tablespoons sugar
1 egg	¼ teaspoon cinnamon

Sift together flour, baking powder, salt, and sugar; add egg well beaten, milk, and shortening; beat well, and spread in a greased pan, having mixture about an inch deep; core, pare, and quarter apples, cut in thick slices, and arrange in rows on top of cake; sprinkle with sugar and cinnamon, and bake in hot oven half an hour. Serve with liquid sauce.

540.—STEAMED APPLE PUDDING

6 apples	3 teaspoons baking powder
½ cup sugar	½ teaspoon salt
½ teaspoon nutmeg	2 tablespoons shortening
1½ cups flour	¾ cup milk

Pare, core, and slice apples; place in a greased pudding dish, and sprinkle with sugar and nutmeg mixed. Sift flour, baking powder, and salt; rub in shortening with finger tips, and mix with milk; spread over apples, and steam for one hour. Turn out of dish, and serve with apples on top. Serve with Soft Sauce (see No. 617).

541.—BANANA TOAST

Mash and sweeten bananas, heap on rounds of buttered toast, and heat in oven. Serve hot with cream or rich milk. Garnish with split cherries, nuts, or bits of jelly.

542.—BLACKBERRY PUDDING

Add one cup of blackberries to recipe for Cottage Pudding (see No. 549) and serve with Blackberry Sauce (see No. 618).

543.—BLUEBERRY PUDDING

To recipe for Cottage Pudding (see No. 549) add one cup of blueberries.

544.—BROWN BETTY

2 cups soft bread crumbs	¼ teaspoon clove
4 tablespoons butter	¼ teaspoon nutmeg
4 apples	2 tablespoons molasses
1/3 cup brown sugar	2 tablespoons hot water
½ teaspoon cinnamon	¼ teaspoon salt

Mix crumbs with melted butter; pare, core, and slice apples; mix sugar and spices; arrange crumbs and apple in layers in a greased baking dish, sprinkle each layer with sugar; mix molasses, water, and salt, and pour over all. Bake slowly for an hour and a half.

545.—BAKED CRANBERRY PUDDING

2 cups soft bread crumbs   1 cup sugar
¼ cup butter   ½ cup sultana raisins
1 cup chopped cranberries ¼ cup boiling water

Mix crumbs with melted butter; add cranberries, sugar, and raisins, and put into a greased baking dish; add water, and bake in a slow oven one hour. Serve with Soft Sauce (see No. 617).

546.—BAKED INDIAN PUDDING

2 cups boiling water   3 cups hot milk
1 teaspoon salt   ¼ cup molasses
5 tablespoons fine corn meal ½ teaspoon ginger

Add salt to boiling water, sift in corn meal very slowly, and boil ten minutes, stirring often; add milk, molasses, and ginger, pour into a greased earthen dish, and bake very slowly for three hours. Serve with rich milk, cream, or Ginger Sauce (see No. 611).

547.—CARAMEL TOAST PUDDING

¾ cup sugar   ¼ teaspoon salt
2 slices toast   ½ teaspoon nutmeg
2 cups hot milk   1 egg
1 tablespoon butter

Caramelize sugar; cut each slice of toast in quarters, dip in caramel, and arrange in baking dish; add milk to caramel remaining in pan, and stir until dissolved; add butter, salt, nutmeg, and egg slightly beaten; pour over toast, and bake in slow oven about half an hour. Serve with cream, rich milk, or liquid sauce.

548.—STEAMED CHOCOLATE PUDDING

½ cup sugar   1 cup flour

1 tablespoon melted butter 1½ teaspoons baking powder
1 beaten egg   ½ teaspoon cinnamon
½ cup milk   1 square melted chocolate
1/8 teaspoon salt

Mix in order given, put in pudding mold, cover closely, and steam one hour. Serve with cream or Soft Sauce (see No. 617).

549.—COTTAGE PUDDING

¼ cup shortening 2 cups flour
½ cup sugar   4 teaspoons baking powder
1 egg   ¼ teaspoon salt
¾ cup milk

Cream the butter; add the sugar and the well-beaten egg, and beat well; add the milk and then the flour, baking powder, and salt, which have been sifted together; beat again, and bake in hot oven in pudding dish about half an hour, or in individual tins about twenty minutes. Serve with hot liquid sauce.

550.—STEAMED FIG PUDDING

½ cup shortening   1 teaspoon cinnamon
½ cup sugar   ½ teaspoon nutmeg
1 egg well beaten   ½ teaspoon salt
1 cup milk   1 pound figs chopped
½ cup molasses   ¼ cup currants
2½ cups flour   ½ cup flour
5 teaspoons baking powder

Mix shortening and sugar, and beat until creamy; add egg, milk, and molasses, add two and a half cups of flour sifted with baking powder, spices, and salt; beat well; add figs and currants mixed with one-half cup of flour. Pour into a greased mold, and steam three hours, or pour into greased one-pound baking powder boxes, and steam an hour and three-quarters. Serve with Cranberry Sauce (see No. 606) or Currant Jelly Sauce (see No. 608). This pudding keeps well and can be reheated in the top of the double boiler.

551.—STEAMED FRUIT PUDDING

1 egg well beaten	½ teaspoon salt
1 cup molasses	1 teaspoon cinnamon
½ cup water	¼ teaspoon clove
2 tablespoons melted shortening	½ teaspoon mace
1½ cups flour	¾ cup raisins seeded and chopped
½ teaspoon soda	¼ cup currants

Mix egg, molasses, water, and shortening; add dry ingredients sifted together; add fruit; mix well, pour into greased one-pound baking powder boxes, and steam an hour and three-quarters. Serve with a tart sauce. One cup of dates, stoned and cut in pieces, may be used instead of raisins and currants.

552.—MOCK INDIAN PUDDING

2 slices bread buttered	1/3 cup sugar
2 cups milk	¼ teaspoon cinnamon
½ cup molasses	¼ teaspoon salt

Butter two slices bread cut three-quarters of an inch thick, put into buttered baking dish, and pour over the bread the rest of the ingredients mixed together. Bake one and a half hours in a slow oven.

553.—INDIAN TAPIOCA PUDDING

1/3 cup pearl tapioca	½ cup molasses
2 cups boiling water	1 tablespoon butter
1½ teaspoons salt	¼ teaspoon cinnamon

¼ cup corn meal   3 cups hot milk

Soak tapioca in cold water for one hour, and drain; add salt to boiling water, sift in corn meal, and boil ten minutes, stirring often; add tapioca and other ingredients, pour into a greased earthen dish, and bake slowly for two hours.

554.—PEACH DUMPLINGS

Cover halves of preserved peaches with Shortcake Dough (see No. 441) rolled thin; bake in hot oven, and serve with hot peach sirup and hard sauce.

555.—BAKED RICE CUSTARD

1 cup cooked rice   Pinch of salt
2 eggs   1½ cups milk
1/3 cup sugar   ½ teaspoon lemon extract

Mix in order given and bake about twenty minutes in a moderate oven. Serve hot or cold with cream or rich milk.

556.—BAKED RICE PUDDING

½ cup rice   ½ teaspoon salt
2 cups milk   ½ nutmeg grated
2 cups boiling water 1 cup raisins seeded and chopped
¼ cup sugar

Wash rice, mix with other ingredients, pour into a greased baking dish, and bake slowly for three hours. Stir occasionally during first hour of baking to prevent rice and fruit from settling. Serve with rich milk or cream.

557.—MULLED RICE

COLD DESSERTS

558.—BANANA ROYAL

4 bananas	¼ cup powdered sugar
¼ cup currant jelly	4 slices of French Toast (see No. 467) or stale sponge cake

Force bananas and jelly through potato ricer or a sieve, add sugar, and heap on French toast or sponge cake. Or line individual glasses with lady fingers and fill with banana mixture.

559.—BANANA WHIP

4 bananas	4 tablespoons powdered sugar
4 tablespoons grape juice or jelly	Whites of 2 eggs

Peel and scrape bananas, force through a sieve; add grape juice, sugar, and stiffly beaten whites of eggs; pile lightly in individual glass dishes, garnish with bits of jelly, and serve at once. All materials should be very cold.

560.—BANANA AND GRAPE JUICE JELLY

½ box gelatine	¼ cup strained lemon juice
½ cup grape juice	¾ cup sugar
2½ cups boiling water	2 large bananas

Soak gelatine in grape juice five minutes; dissolve in boiling water, add lemon juice and sugar. When jelly begins to stiffen, beat with egg beater, and add the bananas pressed through a sieve.

561.—BLACKBERRY MOLD

1 quart blackberries 2 cups water
½ cup sugar ¾ cup farina
¼ teaspoon salt

Heat berries, sugar, salt, and water, and when boiling add farina slowly. Cook over hot water half an hour, turn into a mold, and serve cold with cream. Blueberries, either fresh or canned, may be used in place of blackberries.

562.—CHARLOTTE RUSSE FILLING

1½ cups thin cream ¼ cup hot milk
1½ teaspoons gelatine 3 tablespoons powdered sugar
2 tablespoons cold milk ½ teaspoon vanilla

Whip the cream with a whip churn; skim off the froth as it rises, and place in a fine sieve to drain; soak gelatine in cold milk, dissolve in hot milk, add sugar and flavoring. Stir occasionally until mixture begins to stiffen; then fold in the whip from the cream.

563.—CHOCOLATE BLANCMANGE

2 cups hot milk ¼ cup sugar
4 tablespoons cornstarch 1½ squares chocolate melted
¼ teaspoon salt Whites 2 eggs
¼ teaspoon cinnamon

Scald milk; mix cornstarch, salt, cinnamon, and sugar; add slowly to milk, and cook over hot water until thickened, stirring constantly; add chocolate and cook for fifteen minutes, stirring occasionally; fold in the stiffly beaten whites of eggs, and turn into individual molds to chill.

564.—COCONUT AND ORANGE JELLY

½ box gelatine   1/3 cup sugar
½ cup cold water   1 can coconut
1 cup hot milk   Cold milk
¼ cup orange marmalade

Soak gelatine in cold water for five minutes; dissolve in hot milk; add marmalade and sugar; drain one can of coconut, and add to coconut milk enough cold milk to make one and a half cups; mix with jelly, add coconut, and pour into a mold to chill.

565.—COFFEE CARAMEL CUSTARDS

½ cup sugar   2 eggs
1 cup milk   Few grains salt
1 cup strong coffee

Put sugar in smooth saucepan, and stir over fire until a light-colored caramel is formed. (Avoid burning.) Heat milk and coffee, add to caramel, and keep over hot water until caramel is dissolved; add eggs slightly beaten and salt; strain into cups, and bake in slow oven until firm.

566.—COFFEE JUNKET

2 cups lukewarm milk   Few grains salt
¼ cup sugar   ½ junket tablet
1 teaspoon instantaneous coffee   1 teaspoon cold water

Mix milk, sugar, coffee, and salt; stir until sugar is dissolved; dissolve junket tablet in cold water, add to milk, and pour into glasses. If milk is overheated junket will not be firm.

567.—CRANBERRY WHIP

Follow recipe for Prune Whip (see No. 574), using one cup of strained cranberry sauce instead of prunes.

568.—SOFT CUSTARD

2 cups milk   Few grains salt
Yolks of 2 eggs   1 teaspoon cornstarch
¼ cup sugar   ½ teaspoon vanilla

Scald the milk; mix sugar, salt, and cornstarch, add to beaten egg yolks, and stir into the hot milk; cook over hot water ten minutes, stirring constantly until thickened; beat with egg beater; strain, cool, and add vanilla. To vary the flavor, the sugar may be caramelized, or other extracts may be used. Serve in glasses with a meringue made of the whites of eggs beaten stiff and sweetened with two tablespoons of sugar. Garnish with dots of red jelly.

569.—COFFEE AND RICE JELLY

½ box gelatine   1 cup milk
½ cup cold coffee   ¾ cup sugar
2 cups hot strong coffee   1 cup cooked rice

Soak gelatine in cold coffee five minutes; add hot coffee and stir until dissolved; add milk and sugar; chill, and, when beginning to stiffen, beat with egg beater, add rice, and turn into a mold.

570.—FRUIT CREAM

2 bananas   1 tablespoon granulated gelatine
1 orange   ¼ cup boiling water
½ lemon   1 cup cream whipped
1/3 cup powdered sugar

Press bananas through a sieve; add juice and pulp of orange, juice of lemon, sugar, and gelatine which has been dissolved in hot water. Stir over ice water until mixture begins to stiffen, then fold in the cream. Put in mold and chill.

571.—SPICED FRUIT JELLY

6 apples
½ cup cranberries
¾ cup boiling water
1 cup sugar
1 tablespoon gelatine
¼ cup cold water
½ teaspoon cinnamon
¼ teaspoon clove

Core and slice apples, and cook with cranberries and boiling water fifteen minutes; press through a sieve, add sugar, gelatine dissolved in cold water, and spice. Stir until sugar is dissolved, pour into a mold, and put in a cool place until firm.

572.—FRUIT WHIP (Uncooked)

4 tart apples grated
4 figs chopped
8 dates stoned and chopped
2 tablespoons fruit jelly
Whites of 2 eggs

Mix fruit; mash jelly with a fork; add to fruit, and fold in the stiffly beaten whites of eggs. Serve in glasses, and garnish with bits of jelly.

573.—PINEAPPLE PUDDING

Follow recipe for Chocolate Blancmange (see No. 563), omitting chocolate and cinnamon, and adding one-half can of grated pineapple.

574.—PRUNE WHIP

Press cooked and stoned prunes through a sieve; to one cup of prune pulp add two tablespoons of sugar; beat the whites of two eggs very stiff; add prune mixture gradually, and beat well with a strong egg beater; when light turn into a small greased baking dish or into four individual dishes, and bake in a slow oven about twenty minutes, or until firm. Serve plain or with a custard sauce made from the yolks of the eggs.

575.—PRUNE AND WHEAT MOLD

1 cup prunes   ¼ teaspoon salt
Boiling water ½ cup Cream of Wheat

Wash prunes, soak over night; cook in same water until tender, and remove the stones; measure prunes and juice, and add boiling water to make one quart; add salt; slowly sift in wheat, and cook over hot water for half an hour, stirring often at first; turn into a mold to cool.

576.—JELLIED PRUNES AND CRANBERRIES

1 cup prunes   1 cup sugar
Boiling water   ½ box gelatine
1 cup cranberries chopped ½ cup cold water

Wash prunes, and soak over night in water to cover; cook until soft in same water; drain, measure juice, and add enough boiling water to make three cups; put cranberries in a colander and rinse off the seeds with running water; drain, and add to water; add sugar, and cook ten minutes; add the gelatine soaked in cold water; stone the prunes, cut in quarters, and add to cranberries; turn into a mold, and chill.

577.—RICE MOLD

1 cup rice   Grated rind of ½ orange
2 quarts boiling water ¾ cup powdered sugar
1 tablespoon salt   2 tablespoons grape juice
Juice of 1 orange

Cook rice in boiling salted water until tender; drain; mix with orange, sugar, and grape juice; press into a mold, and chill; turn out of mold, and serve with cream.

578.—SEA MOSS BLANCMANGE

FROZEN DESSERTS

579.—TO FREEZE ICES

Use one measure of freezing salt to three measures of finely cracked ice for ice cream, sherbet, and all mixtures which are to be churned. Freeze slowly, remove dasher, pack solidly, add fresh salt and ice, and let stand for an hour before serving. To freeze mousse, bombe, and all unchurned mixtures, pack in equal parts of salt and ice, and let stand three hours.

580.—FROZEN CUSTARD

    1 quart milk 2 teaspoons cornstarch
    2 eggs   1 tablespoon vanilla
    1 cup sugar Few grains salt

Scald milk; beat eggs slightly, add sugar mixed with cornstarch, and stir into milk; cook over hot water for twelve minutes, stirring constantly at first. Cool, add vanilla and salt, and freeze. Part cream may be used to advantage, or one can of evaporated milk with enough fresh milk added to make one quart.

581.—CHOCOLATE ICE CREAM

Follow recipe for Vanilla Ice Cream (see No. 589), adding two and a half squares of chocolate to the custard before cooking.

582.—COCOA ICE CREAM

    1 pint milk   1 teaspoon cornstarch

2 inches stick cinnamon 1 egg beaten
1 cup sugar 1 pint cream
½ cup cocoa 1 teaspoon vanilla
Few grains salt

Scald milk with cinnamon; mix sugar, cocoa, salt, cornstarch, and egg, and cook with milk until slightly thickened; cool, remove cinnamon, add cream and vanilla, and freeze.

583.—COFFEE ICE CREAM

1 can evaporated milk ½ cup sugar
1 cup boiling water 2 teaspoons instantaneous coffee

Add boiling water to milk, and cool; add sugar and flavoring, and freeze. Serve in glasses and garnish with whipped cream.

584.—MINT ICE CREAM

1 quart thin cream White of 1 egg
½ pound mint stick candy

Put half of cream in double boiler with candy, and heat until candy is dissolved. Cool, add the remainder of cream whipped, and the white of egg beaten stiff; freeze; and serve in glasses garnished with small green mint candies.

585.—ORANGE VELVET CREAM

1 cup sugar 1 cup orange juice
1 cup water Juice of 1 lemon
Whites of 2 eggs 1 pint cream whipped

Boil sugar and water until it threads; cool slightly and add gradually to the stiffly beaten whites of eggs, beating steadily for three minutes; add fruit juice, and when cool fold in cream. Freeze, and serve in glasses garnished with candied orange peel and a few mint leaves.

586.—PHILADELPHIA ICE CREAM

    1 quart thin cream Few grains salt
    ¾ cup sugar   1 tablespoon flavoring

Mix and freeze.

587.—PRUNE ICE CREAM

    1½ cups hot milk   1 cup cream
    2 eggs slightly beaten 2 cups cooked prunes
    ½ cup brown sugar

Cook milk, eggs, and sugar over hot water until thickened, stirring constantly; when cool add cream, prunes stoned and pressed through a sieve, and freeze. Undiluted, unsweetened, evaporated milk may be used in place of cream.

588.—STRAWBERRY ICE CREAM

    1 quart strawberries 1 quart thin cream
    1½ cups sugar

Mash strawberries, add sugar, let stand an hour, and press through a sieve; add cream, and freeze.

589.—VANILLA ICE CREAM

    1 pint milk Few grains salt
    1 cup sugar 1 pint cream
    2 eggs   1 tablespoon vanilla

Scald milk, add sugar, salt, and eggs slightly beaten; cook over hot water until mixture coats spoon; cool; add cream and vanilla, and freeze.

590.—CANTON GINGER SHERBET

½ cup Canton ginger   Juice of 1 orange
1 cup sugar   Juice of ½ lemon
3½ cups boiling water   White of 1 egg

Put ginger through the food chopper, using finest cutter; add sugar and water, and boil fifteen minutes; add fruit juice; cool, and freeze. When nearly frozen, add the stiffly beaten white of egg.

591.—CIDER FRAPPÉ

1 quart sweet cider   Juice of 3 oranges
1 cup sugar   Juice of 1 lemon

Mix cider, sugar, and strained fruit juice; freeze to a mush, and serve in frappé glasses with the roast.

592.—CRANBERRY AND RAISIN SHERBET

3 cups cranberries   1½ cups sugar
1 cup seeded raisins   White of 1 egg
1½ cups water

Cook cranberries, raisins, and water ten minutes; press through a sieve, add sugar, and freeze; when nearly frozen add the stiffly beaten white of egg, and continue freezing until stiff and smooth.

593.—FRUIT SHERBET

1 cup sugar   Juice of 1 orange
1 cup water   Juice of 1 lemon

1 teaspoon gelatine ¾ cup grated pineapple
2 tablespoons cold water 1 banana peeled and mashed

Boil sugar and water five minutes, add gelatine soaked in cold water, and stir until dissolved; add fruit; cool, and freeze.

594.—GRAPE BOMBE

Line a mold with Grape Sherbet (see No. 595), fill with Charlotte Russe Filling (see No. 562) to within one inch of top, cover with sherbet, and pack in salt and ice for three hours.

595.—GRAPE SHERBET

1 cup sugar   2 tablespoons water
1 cup water   1 cup grape juice
1 teaspoon gelatine Juice of 1 lemon

Boil sugar and water five minutes; soak gelatine in cold water five minutes and add to sirup; add fruit juice, cool, and freeze. Serve in glasses with or without whipped cream garnish.

596.—JELLY SHERBET

1 teaspoon gelatine 1½ cups boiling water
½ cup cold water   White of 1 egg
2 glasses jelly

Put gelatine and cold water in the top of double boiler; let stand five minutes; add jelly and boiling water, and stir until jelly is dissolved; when cool, freeze; when nearly frozen add the stiffly beaten white of egg. This is economical if home made jelly can be used.

597.—PINEAPPLE SHERBET

2/3 cup sugar   Juice of 1 lemon
2 cups boiling water White of 1 egg
½ can grated pineapple

Boil sugar and water for fifteen minutes, add pineapple, and lemon juice; when cool, freeze; when nearly frozen add the stiffly beaten white of egg, and finish freezing.

598.—SOMERSET SHERBET

1 banana   1 cup sugar
½ can apricots, or   1 teaspoon gelatine
1½ cups stewed dried apricots   ¼ cup cold water
1 lemon   1 cup boiling water
1 orange

Press banana and apricots, with their juice, through a sieve; add juice of lemon and orange, and sugar; soak gelatine in cold water, dissolve in boiling water, add to fruit, cool, and freeze.

599.—STRAWBERRY SHERBET

2 cups water   1 box strawberries
1 cup sugar   White of 1 egg

Boil sugar and water five minutes; mash berries, add to sirup, cool, and freeze; when nearly frozen add the stiffly beaten white of egg. If preferred, strain before freezing.

600.—FROZEN WATERMELON

Scoop out the inside of a watermelon with a large spoon; put in the freezer without the dasher, sprinkle with powdered sugar and lemon juice, and pack in equal parts of salt and ice for three hours.

SAUCES FOR DESSERTS

601.—CARAMEL SAUCE

Melt one cup of sugar in a smooth, clean saucepan, add three-fourths cup of boiling water, and simmer fifteen minutes. Take care that sugar does not burn. Strong coffee may be used instead of water, and, if desired, one-half cup of chopped nut meats may be added.

602.—CHOCOLATE SAUCE (Hot)

¾ cup sugar
1/3 cup boiling water
1/8 teaspoon salt
1 square chocolate
2 teaspoons boiling water
1 teaspoon butter
½ teaspoon vanilla

Cook sugar, one-third cup water, salt, and chocolate until sirup threads; remove from fire, add two teaspoons water, butter, and vanilla.

603.—CHOCOLATE MARSHMALLOW SAUCE

1 square chocolate
½ tablespoon butter
1 tablespoon flour
Few grains salt
¼ cup sugar
1 cup boiling water
8 marshmallows cut in pieces
½ teaspoon vanilla

Melt chocolate; add butter, flour, salt, sugar, and mix well; add water and boil two minutes; add marshmallows and beat well; add vanilla and serve hot. One tablespoon of shredded almonds may be added; or the marshmallows may be omitted and two tablespoons each of chopped nuts and raisins added.

604.—CINNAMON SAUCE

Use recipe for Lemon Sauce (see No. 613); but omit the lemon flavoring, and add one teaspoon cinnamon and one tablespoon of molasses.

605.—COFFEE SAUCE (Evaporated Milk)

1 cup evaporated milk 1 teaspoon soluble coffee, or
¼ cup sugar   2 tablespoons clear black coffee

Place milk on ice for a few hours; beat with a rotary egg beater until stiff, add sugar and flavoring.

606.—CRANBERRY SAUCE (Pudding)

¼ cup butter   2 tablespoons boiling water
1 cup powdered sugar   ½ cup strained cranberry sauce

Cream butter, add sugar and water gradually and alternately; beat well, and add cranberry sauce. The stiffly beaten white of one egg may be added. Serve with cottage or steamed puddings.

607.—CUSTARD SAUCE

Make the same as Soft Custard (see No. 568).

608.—CURRANT JELLY SAUCE (Pudding)

1 tablespoon cornstarch 2 tablespoons currant jelly
¼ cup sugar   1 teaspoon butter
1 cup boiling water   Juice of ½ lemon

Mix cornstarch and sugar in a saucepan, add water gradually, when thickened add jelly, simmer ten minutes; add butter and lemon juice just before serving.

609.—DATE SAUCE

To Lemon Sauce (see No. 613) add eight dates, which have been washed, stoned, and cut in small pieces. Serve with Cottage Pudding (see No. 549).

610.—FRUIT SAUCE

Heat one cup of sirup of preserved or canned fruit, thicken with one teaspoon of cornstarch moistened with one tablespoon of cold water, and cook ten minutes; add a few grains of salt, a teaspoon of butter, a few drops of red coloring, and serve hot.

611.—GINGER SAUCE

½ cup sugar 2 tablespoons water
¼ cup molasses 2 tablespoons vinegar
1 teaspoon butter ½ tablespoon ginger

Mix in order given, boil for five minutes, and serve hot with Indian Pudding (see No. 553) or Steamed Fruit Pudding (see No. 551).

612.—HARD SAUCE

¼ cup butter 1 teaspoon vanilla, or
1 cup powdered sugar ¼ teaspoon nutmeg
1 teaspoon milk

Cream butter, add sugar and milk gradually, and beat until very light; add flavoring, and chill before serving.

613.—LEMON SAUCE

¾ cup sugar 1 teaspoon butter
2 teaspoons cornstarch Juice and rind of ½ lemon, or
1/8 teaspoon salt ½ teaspoon lemon extract
1½ cups hot water

Mix sugar, cornstarch, and salt; add hot water, stir constantly until boiling point is reached, and simmer ten minutes; add butter and flavoring. One teaspoon of vanilla or one-half nutmeg grated may be used instead of lemon.

614.—MARSHMALLOW SAUCE

1 cup sugar 1 cup marshmallows
½ cup boiling water ½ teaspoon vanilla

Boil sugar and water five minutes, add marshmallows, beat until they are melted, and add vanilla. Beat well before serving. Serve hot or cold.

615.—MOCHA SAUCE

¼ cup butter or Crisco 1 teaspoon powdered soluble coffee
1 cup powdered sugar 1 tablespoon cocoa
2 tablespoons milk

Cream shortening, add sugar and milk gradually, and beat until light; add coffee and cocoa, and blend well.

616.—ORANGE MARMALADE SAUCE

½ cup orange marmalade ½ cup boiling water
½ tablespoon butter

Mix and serve hot with Cottage Pudding (see No. 549), steamed puddings, or griddle cakes.

617.—SOFT SAUCE

To Hard Sauce (see No. 612) add two tablespoons of hot milk, a few drops at a time; beat well, and do not chill.

618.—STRAWBERRY SAUCE

2 tablespoons butter   2 tablespoons boiling water
¾ cup powdered sugar 1 cup crushed strawberries

Cream butter, add half of sugar gradually; add remaining half of sugar alternately with the water; beat well, and add strawberries. Blackberries or raspberries may be used instead of strawberries.

PASTRIES

619.—PLAIN PASTE

1½ cups flour   ¼ cup shortening
¼ teaspoon salt   1/3 cup ice water
¼ teaspoon baking powder   ¼ cup butter

Sift flour, salt, and baking powder; rub in shortening with finger tips until mixture is like fine meal; add water gradually until a soft but not sticky dough is formed, mixing with a knife; when dough is mixed, the side of the bowl should be clean, neither sticky nor dry with flour. Slightly more or less water may be needed. Roll paste, on a lightly floured board, into an even rectangular shape; divide butter into three parts; cover two-thirds of paste with dots of butter, using one part; fold first the unbuttered third, then the remaining third, so that there will be three layers of paste with butter between; roll out again, dot with butter as before, and fold; repeat for third time. Put paste on ice until thoroughly chilled. Any good shortening may be used in place of butter, but the butter flavor will be lacking. This is enough for one pie with two crusts; double the amount of paste can be made with the same amount of labor. It keeps well if wrapped in cheesecloth and put in a cool place.

620.—RICH PASTE

3 cups flour   1¼ cups shortening
1 teaspoon sugar   1 tablespoon lemon juice
½ teaspoon salt   Ice water

Sift flour, sugar, and salt; add shortening, and rub in with finger tips or chop with a knife in each hand until mixture is like fine meal; add lemon juice and enough water to form a stiff paste (about two-thirds of a cup); roll out into a thin sheet and fold in four layers; roll out and fold three times. Chill before using. This rule makes two pies. It is less expensive than puff paste, and yet is a very good substitute for it.

621.—PATTY SHELLS

Roll paste one-eighth of an inch thick, cover inverted tin patty pans or individual pie dishes, trim paste evenly, and press down the edge firmly; prick with a fork, place on a baking sheet, and bake in a hot oven about twelve minutes. Remove pans, and fill with any cooked fruit mixture, berries, or creamed meats or vegetables.

622.—PIE SHELL

Roll paste one-quarter inch thick, cover an inverted tin pie plate, trim, and press the edges firmly; prick with a fork, place on a baking sheet, and bake in a hot oven about fifteen minutes. Fill with cooked pie mixtures and cover with a meringue, or garnish with bits of pastry which have been cut in fancy shapes and baked.

623.—TART SHELLS

Roll Rich Paste (see No. 620) one-third of an inch thick, cut into small rounds, moisten the edges of half of them with cold water, cut out the centers of the other half with a small cutter, place upon whole rounds, and press firmly together; chill, and bake in a hot oven about twenty minutes. Fill with jelly, jam, or fruit paste. When shells are to be filled with creamed meats, etc., cut with a larger cutter.

624.—MINCE MEAT

4 cups cooked beef chopped	1 pound citron shredded
2 cups chopped suet	2 tablespoons salt
8 cups chopped apples	1 tablespoon cinnamon

1 cup brown sugar	1 tablespoon mace
2 cups molasses	1 teaspoon clove
1 glass tart jelly	1 teaspoon allspice
1½ pounds seeded raisins	½ teaspoon pepper
1 pound washed currants	1 quart boiled cider

Mix, and cook slowly about two hours, stirring frequently. One cup of chopped cranberries may be substituted for the jelly. Store in jars or in a stone crock. If mince meat grows dry by standing, moisten with a little coffee.

625.—MOCK MINCE MEAT (Uncooked)

1½ cups chopped apples	½ teaspoon cinnamon
¼ cup raisins seeded and chopped	½ teaspoon mace
¼ cup cranberries chopped	¼ teaspoon clove
¼ cup currants	¾ cup brown sugar
1 tablespoon citron shredded	¼ cup vinegar
¼ cup beef fat melted	½ cup coffee
½ teaspoon salt	

Mix in order given and let stand a few hours before using. (Fills one large pie.)

626.—GREEN TOMATO MINCE MEAT

1½ cups green tomatoes chopped	¼ cup water
1½ cups apple chopped	¾ teaspoon cinnamon
¾ cup raisins seeded and chopped	½ teaspoon mace
1 cup brown sugar	¼ teaspoon clove
¼ cup beef fat melted	¾ teaspoon salt
2 tablespoons vinegar	½ cup jelly, fruit sirup, or grape juice

Mix and cook slowly for one hour. (Fills two pies.)

White of 1 egg   1 teaspoon baking powder
½ cup granulated sugar ¼ teaspoon extract

Beat the egg until stiff, add gradually sugar mixed with baking powder, flavor, spread on tarts or pies, and bake in a moderate oven ten minutes.

629.—SLICED APPLE PIE

3½ cups pared and sliced apples 1/8 teaspoon salt
½ cup sugar   1/3 teaspoon nutmeg or cinnamon

Line a plate with paste, fill with apples, mounding them in the center; mix sugar, salt, and seasoning, and cover apples; moisten edge of paste with water; roll out paste for top crust, cut one-half inch larger than plate, and cut a few small gashes in the center; cover pie, turn edge under the lower crust, and press firmly. Brush with milk, and bake about forty minutes. The oven should be hot for the first fifteen minutes, and then the heat should be reduced.

630.—BLUEBERRY PIE

2½ cups blueberries 2½ tablespoons flour
2/3 cup sugar   1 teaspoon butter

Line a pie plate with paste; fill with berries, add sugar and flour mixed, and dot butter over top. Cover, and bake the same as Apple Pie (see No. 629).

631.—CHERRY PIE

Follow recipe for Blueberry Pie (see No. 630), using stoned cherries in place of blueberries and adding one-fourth cup more sugar.

632.—MOCK CHERRY PIE

1½ cups cranberries chopped and rinsed 1 cup sugar

½ cup raisins seeded and chopped   ½ cup water
2 tablespoons sifted crumbs or flour

Mix, and bake in two crusts, the same as Apple Pie (see No. 629).

633.—CRANBERRY PIE

2 cups cranberries   2 tablespoons sifted crumbs
1¼ cups sugar   ½ cup hot water

Chop cranberries, rinse, and mix with sugar, crumbs, and water. Roll paste one-quarter inch thick, cover a perforated tin plate, trim the edge evenly, and moisten edge with water; fill with cranberries, cover with half-inch strips of paste placed half an inch apart to form a lattice top; trim the edges neatly, moisten, and finish with a half-inch strip of paste around the edge. Bake about forty minutes. The oven should be hot for the first fifteen minutes, and then the heat should be reduced.

634.—OPEN CRANBERRY PIE

1½ cups cranberries   2/3 cup water
1 cup sugar   2 tablespoons sifted crumbs

Mix berries, sugar, and water, and cook for ten minutes, stirring frequently to break the berries; add crumbs, and when nearly cool pour into a baked pie shell. Garnish with bits of baked pastry.

635.—CUSTARD PIE (Cake Crumbs)

2 cups hot milk   1 egg slightly beaten
½ cup dry cake crumbs   1/8 teaspoon salt
2 tablespoons sugar   Nutmeg

Mix crumbs and milk, let stand for five minutes, and press through a sieve; add sugar, egg, and salt; line a deep plate with paste rolled thin; build up a firm edge of crust, fill with custard, and dust with nutmeg. Bake about forty minutes. The oven should be hot for the first ten minutes, and then the heat should be reduced.

636.—GOOSEBERRY PIE

To recipe for Gooseberry Patties (see No. 648) add two tablespoons of dried and sifted crumbs. Prepare and bake the same as Cranberry Pie (see No. 633).

637.—LEMON PIE

1 slice bread one inch thick	Yolks 2 eggs
1 cup boiling water	1/8 teaspoon salt
1 cup sugar	Rind and juice 1 lemon

Remove crusts from bread; cover bread with boiling water, let stand a few minutes, and press through a sieve; add sugar, egg yolks slightly beaten, salt, lemon rind, and lemon juice. Prepare paste, fill, and bake the same as Custard Pie (see No. 635). Make a Meringue (see No. 627) of the whites of eggs.

638.—MARLBOROUGH PIE

6 apples	Grated rind and juice 1 lemon
1/3 cup sugar	1 teaspoon cinnamon
2 macaroons rolled	¼ teaspoon salt
2 tablespoons butter	2 eggs slightly beaten

Pare and slice apples, add one-quarter cup of water; cook until soft, and rub through a sieve; add other ingredients in order given. Line a deep plate or patty tins with rich paste, fill, and bake about forty minutes. Cake crumbs may be substituted for macaroons.

639.—MINCE PIE

Line a perforated tin plate with paste, rolled one-fourth inch thick; fill with mince meat, moisten edges with water, and cover with an upper crust with a few small gashes cut in it; turn the edge under lower crust about half an inch, press firmly, and trim edges of paste with a knife, slanting toward the center; brush with milk, and bake in a hot oven about half an hour.

640.—ORANGE PIE

1½ cups hot milk   Juice of 1 orange
½ cup cake crumbs   1 egg slightly beaten
½ cup sugar   1/8 teaspoon salt
Grated rind of ½ orange

Mix milk and crumbs, let stand five minutes, and press through a fine sieve; add other ingredients. Prepare paste, fill, and bake the same as Custard Pie (see No. 635).

641.—PINEAPPLE PIE

1 can grated pineapple   Few grains salt
1 cup sugar   1 egg
2½ tablespoons flour   ½ tablespoon butter

Mix sugar, flour, and salt, add beaten egg, and mix with pineapple; pour into a deep pie plate lined with paste, add butter in small pieces, cover with strips of paste, and bake in a hot oven about forty minutes, reducing the heat during second half of baking.

642.—PRUNE PIE

2 cups cooked prunes   1 tablespoon flour
½ cup sugar   Grated rind of ½ orange

Stone prunes, cut in quarters, and put into a paste-lined plate; cover with sugar, flour, and rind mixed. Cover with upper crust, brush with milk, and bake in a hot oven half an hour, reducing the heat during second half of baking.

643.—PUMPKIN PIE

1½ cups baked pumpkin ½ teaspoon ginger
1 egg well beaten   1 teaspoon cinnamon
2/3 cup brown sugar   ½ teaspoon cornstarch
½ teaspoon salt   1½ cups milk

Cut pumpkin in pieces and bake in a hot oven; mash and strain, and to one and a half cups add the other ingredients in order given. Prepare paste and bake the same as Custard Pie (see No. 635).

644.—RAISIN PIE

½ cup raisins seeded and chopped ¼ cup vinegar
1½ cups hot water   2 tablespoons butter
1 cup brown sugar   ½ cup sifted crumbs

Mix, and cook for ten minutes; cool; and bake the same as Cranberry Pie (see No. 633).

645.—RHUBARB PIE

2 cups rhubarb   1 cup sugar
2 tablespoons sultana raisins Grating of nutmeg
¼ cup sifted crumbs   Few grains salt

Cut rhubarb in half-inch pieces, place in a strainer, and scald with boiling water; drain, put into a paste-lined plate, cover with raisins, crumbs, sugar, and nutmeg and salt mixed; cover with an upper crust, and bake the same as Apple Pie (see No. 629).

646.—SQUASH PIE

1½ cups cooked squash ¼ teaspoon cinnamon
1 cup sugar   ½ teaspoon nutmeg
¾ teaspoon salt   1 egg beaten
¼ cup sifted crumbs 1½ cups milk

Mix in order given. Prepare paste, fill, and bake the same as Custard Pie (see No. 635).

647.—BANBURY TARTS

1 cup raisins Juice and rind of 1 lemon
¾ cup sugar ¼ cup sifted crumbs

Seed and chop raisins, and mix with sugar, lemon, and crumbs. Roll paste one-eighth inch thick, and cut in three-inch rounds; put half a tablespoon of raisin mixture on half of each round, moisten edges with water, fold double, and press edges firmly together. Prick with a fork, and bake in a hot oven about fifteen minutes.

648.—GOOSEBERRY PATTIES

Remove tops and stems from one pint of gooseberries; wash, add one-half cup water, and cook about fifteen minutes, or until soft and well broken; add one cup of sugar, and cool; line patty pans with paste, fill with gooseberries, cover with narrow strips of paste to form a lattice. Bake in a hot oven twenty-five minutes.

649.—PRUNE AND APPLE TART FILLING

Use recipe for Prune and Apple Shortcake (see No. 445), fill cooked paste shells, and garnish with bits of cooked paste.

650.—PRUNE PATTIES

Line patty pans with paste; prepare filling as for Prune Pie (see No. 642); mix, and fill pans; cover with a lattice-work of narrow strips of paste, and finish with a narrow strip of paste around the outer edge. Bake in a hot oven about twenty-five minutes.

651.—INDIVIDUAL RASPBERRY PIE

Roll paste one-eighth inch thick, cut into circles two and a half inches in diameter. Put a tablespoon of raspberry jam on half of them, and moisten the edges with water. With a small round cutter make three holes in each remaining circle, place on top of jam, press edges firmly together, and bake about fifteen minutes in a hot oven. Bake the small cut-out pieces of paste, and serve with soup.

652.—RHUBARB MERINGUE PATTIES

2 cups rhubarb 1 egg yolk beaten
¼ cup water 3 tablespoons sifted crumbs
1 cup sugar 1 teaspoon butter

Cut rhubarb in half-inch pieces and cook with water ten minutes; add sugar, egg yolk, crumbs, and butter, and cook five minutes; when cool, fill Patty Shells (see No. 621), cover with One-egg Meringue (see No. 628), and bake ten minutes in a moderate oven.

653.—SQUASH PATTIES (without Eggs)

2 cups cooked and sifted squash 1 tablespoon dried and sifted crumbs
½ cup sugar ½ teaspoon lemon extract
2/3 teaspoon salt

Mix in order given. Line patty pans with paste, fill with squash, and bake in a hot oven about twenty-five minutes.

654.—CHEESE STRAWS

½ cup flour	1/8 teaspoon mustard
1 tablespoon shortening	¼ teaspoon paprika
¼ cup grated cheese	¼ teaspoon baking powder
1/8 teaspoon salt	Ice water

Rub shortening into flour with finger tips; add cheese, seasonings, and baking powder, and mix to a stiff dough with ice water. Roll out, fold in four layers, roll out again and fold as before; put on ice to chill; roll out one-third inch thick, and cut into four-inch straws. Bake in a hot oven about twelve minutes.

655.—CHEESE STRAWS (Left-over Paste)

Roll trimmings of pastry into a thin sheet, sprinkle with grated cheese and paprika; fold in four layers; repeat; chill, cut into straws, and bake in a hot oven about twelve minutes.

656.—CHEESE WAFERS

Prepare paste as for Cheese Straws (see No. 654); roll out very thin, cut with a two-inch cutter, and bake in a hot oven about six minutes.

657.—CINNAMON HEARTS

Roll Rich Paste (see No. 620) very thin in an even rectangular shape; sprinkle with powdered sugar mixed with a little cinnamon. The paste should be about twelve inches long. Fold each end toward the center two inches; fold each end again toward the center; fold double, and chill. Cut in one-third-inch slices, place flat side down on a baking sheet two inches apart, and bake in a hot oven about eight minutes.

www.ingramcontent.com/pod-product-compliance
Lightning Source LLC
Chambersburg PA
CBHW081622100526
44590CB00021B/3557